ROVING THROUGH SOUTHERN CHINA

Harry Alverson Franck was born in 1881 in Michigan. His lifelong wanderlust seems to have set in early. He left to see Europe in 1900, working his passage across the Atlantic on a cattle boat. After graduating, he spent 16 months circling the globe. He walked across the Malay peninsula to some press attention. His initial East Asian travels were recounted in *Wandering in Northern China* (1923). He then travelled to Japan and Taiwan for *Glimpses of Japan and Formosa* (1924), before heading to Canton, Hong Kong and Macao for *Roving Through Southern China* (1925). Franck sent despatches to American newspapers as he travelled to ensure an income while on the move. He was often billed as "Harry A Franck – The Prince of Vagabonds".

Paul French, who has introduced and annotated this reprint, was born in London and lived in Shanghai for many years. His book *Midnight in Peking* was a *New York Times* bestseller and a BBC Radio 4 Book of the Week.

Also by Paul French:

Destination Peking

Strangers on the Praia

Destination Shanghai

City of Devils: A Shanghai Noir

Midnight in Peking: How the Murder of a Young Englishwoman Haunted the Last Days of Old Peking

The Badlands: Decadent Playground of Old Peking

Bloody Saturday: Shanghai's Darkest Day

Supreme Leader: The Making of Kim Jong-un

Betrayal in Paris: How the Treaty of Versailles Led to China's Long Revolution

The Old Shanghai A-Z

Through the Looking Glass: China's Foreign Journalists from Opium Wars to Mao

Carl Crow – A Tough Old China Hand: The Life, Times, and Adventures of an American in Shanghai

North Korea Paranoid Peninsula – A Modern History

Roving Through Southern China

An American's Explorations of Hong Kong, Macao and Canton in the Early 1920s

By Harry Franck
(1925)

Annotated by Paul French

BLACKSMITH BOOKS

China Revisited: No. 4 of a series

Roving Through Southern China

ISBN 978-988-76748-3-2

Published by Blacksmith Books
Unit 26, 19/F, Block B, Wah Lok Industrial Centre,
37-41 Shan Mei Street, Fo Tan, Hong Kong
Tel: (+852) 2877 7899
www.blacksmithbooks.com

Foreword and introduction copyright © 2024 Paul French

Cover photograph by G. Warren Swire. Image courtesy of John
Swire & Sons Ltd and Special Collections, University of Bristol
Library (www.hpcbristol.net). Many thanks to Jamie Carstairs and
Robert Bickers of the Historical Photographs of China project at
the University of Bristol.

CONTENTS

ABOUT CHINA REVISITED

China Revisited is a series of extracted reprints of mid-nineteenth to early-twentieth century Western impressions of Hong Kong, Macao and China. The series comprises excerpts from travelogues or memoirs written by missionaries, diplomats, military personnel, journalists, tourists and temporary sojourners. They came to China from Europe or the United States, some to work or to serve the interests of their country, others out of curiosity. Each excerpt is fully annotated to best provide relevant explications of Hong Kong, Macao and China at the time, to illuminate encounters with historically interesting characters or notable events.

Given the prejudices of the era, what are we to take from these works? Some have a stated agenda, namely colonial control and administration of Hong Kong and Macao, or else proselytising and saving souls for the Christian religion. This is generally obvious in the writing. Others have no stated objective but impressions of the regions, their peoples, and cultures are products of their time and value systems. There is an unsurprising tendency to exoticize, make generally unfavourable comparisons to their home cultures and societies, and to misunderstand what they are witnessing.

They are – whether from American or European sources – invariably from men and women of some formal education. Their acquaintances are among the colonial authorities and foreign diplomats. These "filters" mean that invariably we are given an elite view of China; this is not the experience of the non-officer class sailor, merchant seaman, regular soldier, or working-class visitor. Even before we get to racial prejudice we are encountering class prejudice.

The writers in this series were all men and women of their time, encountering China at specific times in its history. Most of them were visitors or residents for a limited amount of time. However, some, notably the missionaries, did remain for longer – decades in some cases. In general the only foreigners who had credible local language skills were the missionaries, or British colonial district officers and their Portuguese equivalents in Macao, along with some diplomat-scholars. Assumptions were made, prejudices voiced, yet all of these writings have something to reveal of the encounters from which they derived.

FOREWORD

"Vagabonding" in Southern China

Harry A Franck's *Roving Through Southern China* was first published in 1925 in the United States by The Century Company of New York and London. However, this text is taken from the British first edition published a year later, in 1926 (and so entered the public domain on January 1, 2022), by T Fisher Unwin based at Adelphi Terrace in London. There were no significant differences between the two editions.

This is an abridged and annotated version of Franck's full book, which is nearly eight hundred pages long. The territory covered by Franck for this volume included the southern part of China, from Shanghai south to Canton (Guangzhou) and across to neighbouring Hong Kong and Macao, with a subsequent tour through the western provinces with stops at Yunnan-fu (Kunming) and Chengtu (Chengdu). The original text includes a map of Franck's journey along with 171 photographs (a very high number of images for the time, as discussed in the brief appendix to this book).

Franck invariably referred to his travels, which had included through French Indochina and across Japan and Korea as "vagabonding", though for some reason (perhaps because he was accompanied by his family) used the alternative term "roving" for this volume as he did spend some settled periods in various locations, including a sojourn in Canton. If nothing else, Franck's account of his travels in southern China are almost unique for the time, being a family adventure – husband, wife, two children and Franck's mother. His extended stay in Canton gave him the chance to explore and write about the environs of the city, particularly the then quite distant Honam Island area (now Guangzhou's Haizhu District).

INTRODUCTION

"The Prince of Vagabonds"

Harry Alverson Franck was born in 1881 in Munger, Michigan into a blacksmithing family originally of German heritage. His lifelong wanderlust seems to have set in early. He left the University of Michigan to see Europe in 1900, working his passage across the Atlantic on a cattle boat. After eventually graduating UMich, and following a short spell teaching to raise funds, Franck spent sixteen months circling the globe. He worked his passage in various ways and walked across the Malay peninsula to some press attention. His recounted these adventures in his first book, *A Vagabond Journey Around the World* (1910).

He returned to the United States to work as a teacher for a couple of years, followed by a stint as a policeman in the Panama Canal Zone, an experience recounted in his book *Zone Policeman 88* (1913). He also journeyed further south and wrote *Vagabonding Down the Andes* (1917). He was deployed to Europe as a lieutenant in the cavalry in World War I following the United States's entry into the conflict. He remained in Europe after the armistice to explore his German roots in *Vagabonding Through Changing Germany* (1920), noting the chaos of the immediate post-World War I era and the country's polarisation between revolutionaries and reactionaries.

His initial East Asian travels were recounted in *Wandering in Northern China* (1923), which included detailed observations of his travels in Manchuria and Korea (the latter then fairly newly under Japanese colonial control). He noted the severe deforestation of the peninsula and that many former Korean nobles had been reduced to living in poverty since the Japanese takeover. On his visit to Manchuria, and in particular Harbin, Franck noted the large number of Russian exiles from the Bolshevik Revolution who had arrived in the city and their general impoverishment. He then travelled to Japan and Taiwan for *Glimpses of Japan and Formosa* (1924), before heading to southern China, Hong Kong and Macao for *Roving Through Southern China* (1925).

He was to maintain an interest in East and Southeast Asia, producing a number of titles including *East of Siam* (1926) and two textbooks: *The Japanese Empire: Geographical Reader* (1927) and *China: Geographical Reader* (1927). He claimed to have visited every one of the (then) eighteen provinces of China on his travels.

In the 1930s Franck went on to spend some time travelling in the Soviet Union and across Alaska. He was re-commissioned in World War II, serving with the Ninth United States Air Force in France.

While serving in France in World War I, Franck had met Rachel Latta, a Philadelphian working in a US Army hospital. They were married in 1919. Rachel frequently travelled with Harry and their five children. She recalled this rather peripatetic life and marriage in her own 1939 book, *I Married a Vagabond*. The family eventually settled in Pennsylvania. Harry Franck died in 1962; Rachel in 1986. Many of Franck's books from the 1920s and 1930s were translated into various languages, including Chinese and Japanese.

***

Franck's journey to southern China was a family affair. Rachel and their two young children (three more would follow later) accompanied him, as did Franck's mother. Indeed, *Roving Through Southern China* is dedicated to his mother – 'Whose only roving was her year with us in southern China'. In his foreword to the book Franck claimed that his route was largely 'random'.

The book in full recounts the period of nearly two years of the Franck family's travels in southern China spanning 1923-1924, arriving back home in December

1924 (his mother, it seems, only stayed for the second year). Partly they sojourned this long because, according to Franck, the modes of transportation available to him at the time were slower than in other parts of East Asia, thus lengthening journey times considerably. Franck was keen to demonstrate that he 'got off the beaten track' while in China, and this certainly was the case in remoter Yunnan province and other places in western China. However, the excerpts here deal with more familiar places – the British colony of Hong Kong, the Portuguese colony of Macao, and the city of Canton (Guangzhou) and its immediate environs.

Franck sent despatches to American newspapers as he travelled to ensure an income while on the move. He was often billed as "Harry A Franck – The Prince of Vagabonds". He was also sending entire manuscripts to his publishers – *Wandering in Northern China* was posted to America and published while Franck was "roving" in southern China already. Presumably he trusted his editors implicitly as it was not possible to undertake the usual back-and-forth of manuscripts given the distances involved and Franck's constant movement. Indeed, Franck appears to have written *Roving Through Southern China* as the family travelled, completing the final manuscript in August 1925 at the Franck family home in Chestnut Hill, northwest Philadelphia. *Roving Through Southern China* was first published the following year. While in America and between journeys Franck maintained a busy schedule of paid speaking engagements detailing his travels to various audiences.

***

So what are we to take from Franck's rovings through southern China and his time in Hong Kong, Macao and around Canton?

Franck passes through Hong Kong at an interesting time, shortly after the long-running and acrimonious Chinese seamen's strike of 1922. He is broadly sympathetic to the strikers and reiterates his view that Hong Kong is held back by the imposition of the British class system and racial prejudices. Certainly the 1922 strike was the most significant industrial action by organised labour that the colonial authorities had had to deal with. Their response fell somewhat short of resolving the deal, which was largely left to the seamen and the ship owners to sort out. The 1922 dispute was of course a precursor to a wave of strikes, boycotts and actions throughout the mid-1920s in Hong Kong and Canton.

Franck is also in Hong Kong at a great time of infrastructural change and notes the mass civil engineering works taking place Kowloon-side with the flattening of mountains and the resultant rubble used for landfill and reclamation to significantly change the dimensions of Kowloon, allow the spread of development north from the tip of the peninsula and eventually reshape Victoria Harbour too.

Arriving in Macao Franck follows the, by then, time-honoured tradition of contrasting the apparent dynamism and commercial verve of British-controlled Hong Kong with the more languid Portuguese-controlled Macao. This notion of Macao as a den of vice, despite its overt Catholicism, was already a familiar trope by the mid-1920s and would only accelerate and become universal in the 1930s. The emphasis on gambling, prostitution and corruption are familiar observations of foreign visitors to Macao at the time and, despite some detailed descriptions of the operations of casinos and fan-tan parlours in Macao, Franck has little different to say. That is, however, perhaps instructive in showing how the repeated and common assumptions about Macao came to define the colony in the interwar years vis-à-vis Hong Kong and southern China.

Franck's descriptions of Canton life are of interest for a number of reasons. Interestingly, and almost uniquely, he is living in the city as a family man, with his wife, children and mother. He is not merely passing through but residing at a time of immense change in the city – structurally and politically. 1922/1923 was a rocky period for Sun Yat-sen's Southern Government, redeveloping the city (Franck laments the knocking down of the old city walls) to create new suburbs and boulevards suitable for a modern city of automobiles, department stores and a new middle class. However, this is also a time of political quarrels, strikes and disturbances, and Franck's detailed descriptions of the foreign enclave of Shameen (Shamian) Island are of interest as it was for much of this time effectively closed off, ringed with barbed wire and isolated, being guarded by foreign troops and gunboats.

Still we glimpse the emergent new Canton of asphalt roads, mass demolition and the removal of the ancient walls (this despite Franck's rant about the backwardness and high cost of Canton's rickshaws). We also see the newly accessible suburbs – Tung Shan, Saikwan, Honam Island. Interestingly Franck and his family are living in the western suburb of Saikwan, not as businesspeople or diplomats but just as residents, observing the minutiae of daily life around them – dried-up creeks, dilapidated rickshaws, noisy construction as well as daily routines including funerals, weddings, cooking, child-rearing and rapid executions of criminals.

Franck's attention is drawn by everyday activities – ivory carving, toothbrush assembly, the manufacture of mah-jongg sets, old lightbulbs converted into small goldfish bowls. He is particularly interesting on the role of women in Canton as mothers, housewives and workers, both in the sampan communities and ashore.

Yet we should remain aware that the Franck family's Canton sojourn was at a troubled time. Sun's government was weak, labour strikes were almost constant, crime was a problem and smallpox was running rampant. Franck's account of his time in the city, as well as his visits to Hong Kong and Macao, are an invaluable insight into daily life in southern China in the tumultuous years of the early 1920s.

Harry A Franck

ROVING THROUGH
SOUTHERN CHINA
(I)

(This text and spellings taken from *Roving Through Southern China, Chapters VIII & IX,* by Harry A Franck, London: T Fisher Unwin Ltd, first British edition, 1926)

LOAFING ALONG THE CHINA COAST
HONG KONG & MACAO

HONG KONG

Hong Kong loomed up through the mists of a late December morning during my second year in China; I was due to pass through it half a dozen times before I left the Orient. Like Shanghai, it had changed much since I first saw it, almost twenty years before. The same funicular cable-cars, however, still carry one to the Peak – so do automobiles also now – to look down upon a scene in a milder way almost as striking as Rio. From the compact narrow city below like the embroidery on the bottom of a skirt the eyes wander away across the deep-blue harbor scattered with scores of ships riding at anchor because the wharves on both sides of the bay are already crowded from end to end with others, merging into islands in the offing that seem likewise anchored in the blue sea, a harbor streaked by constantly arriving and departing steamers from everywhere and by the ferries to the various parts of the mainland suburb of Kowloon, beyond which one may even see hills that are still Chinese.[1]

Hong Kong is not after all in China, though it is not strange that so many people mistake it for a Chinese city. Having taken the island and started the city of Victoria nearly a century ago as a result of the first "opium war," the British were not satisfied until the Chinese gave them a goodly slice of the mainland also; and now they are not satisfied with the way the Lord made what the Chinese gave them, so that slowly the hills of the mainland, as of Hong Kong itself, are being chopped and blasted away to

---

1 It seems that Franck first passed through Hong Kong during his round-the-world trip that began in 1904 and was later published as *A Vagabond Journey Around the World: A Narrative of Personal Experience* (London: T Fisher Unwin, 1910). However, while he details his visits to India, Ceylon (Sri Lanka), Burma (Myanmar), the Kingdom of Siam (Thailand), the Malay peninsula and Japan, he does not include any impressions of Hong Kong in that book.

fill in the hollows and give place to expanding Kowloon and its many suburbs, cluttered with elaborate bamboo scaffolds. These disappearing hills are carried off almost entirely by hand, with long stairways, like the notched stick up which the jungle savage climbs to his dwelling, cut in the steep slopes to give foothold for the Chinese coolies, female as often as male, who do the work.[2] Women with a curious combination of hat and sunshade, of grindstone size and shape with a fringe of black cloth hanging well down about its edge and worn even during midwinter months, carry baskets of stone or earth, or sit breaking rock with a baby or more playing beside them.

Two-storied street-cars, like those of Chile – though here classes are reversed and the haughty white man deigns to ride aloft – move from end to end of the narrow island town, through Happy Valley, promoted now from cemetery to race-track, Kennedy Town, and other sections of British nomenclature; and farther still motor-cars will carry those who can afford them up and over or clear around the steep little island. Motoring is cheaper across the bay, where motor-buses race in constant streams from the ferry-landing to every suburb, and there rickshaws have unlimited scope compared with the little

---

2   Franck regularly uses the term "coolie", a now outdated and offensive pejorative term denoting a low-wage Chinese labourer.

level space in down-town Victoria, behind which the "Do Be Chairful Company" – English wit sieved through Chinese brains comes out in strange forms of facetiousness – provide many clean and comfortable conveyances that are not exactly chairs, though you may sit in them and be carried.[3]

Hong Kong is so free a port that in all the six times I passed through it, two or three times as a family of five with a dozen unassorted pieces of baggage, I was never once spoken to officially, on the question of either passport or baggage. That is what we travelers would have the wide world round, and Hong Kong seems to benefit rather than suffer by it. Looking back upon it I wonder if this Elysian freedom is what I took it to be or merely a sign that no one in official Hong Kong is lowly enough to speak to strangers. Snobbery and the rules of caste taken from one of their chief habitats and marooned on this much tinier island, there to interbreed for generations, not unnaturally have reached heights that emphasize the pettiness of mankind. I never had the experience of a man of my acquaintance who, pausing to ask his way of a passing member of the upper crust in Hong Kong, was violently berated for speaking to him without ever having

---

3   The Do Be Chairful Company did actually exist, with offices at 51 Queen's Road, providing sedan chairs as well as being manufacturers of more static rattan furniture.

been introduced, but I have had hints to convince me that this is not so impossible as it sounds.

That something which even the best of mankind cannot escape when living long among those they consider their inferiors flowers most luxuriantly in small and isolated communities. The character of many a white man in China explains why the effect of slavery was as bad on the slave-owner as on the slave. Our own countrymen in the Orient *(i.e. Americans)* are not free from undemocratic ways; the English in China's large ports are often insufferable even to their fellow-nationals from Canada or Australia. The sleek young fellows who drift down from their residences on the Peak toward ten, half an hour or more later than the signs in their offices announce them, are not seriously to blame for the results of their narrow environment perhaps; but there seems no good reason why older and more traveled men of the same race stationed along the coast of China proper and up the Yang Tze should be still less noted for their civility than their nation as a whole.[4] The unintroduced client is generally greeted with an icy "What can I do for you?" and it is almost the British-Chinese custom to let even a lady stand during the ensuing interview, while the steamship-agent or what not sits tight in the chair from which he did not so much as budge when she entered.

---

4   Yang Tze = Yangtze River.

Even in this tight little British colony Europeans are swamped by the Chinese and their customs. The three-story houses of stucco or cement with heavy overhanging balconies are hung with a vast array of Chinese garments; from the swaying top of a street-car one can look into more Chinese households than into Irish and Italian from the Elevated railway in New York. The complaint is often heard that the Hong Kong Government is really in the hands of the Chinese. The seaman's strike of a few years ago, when the Government that took down their union sign was forced to put it up again with its own fair hands, was a particular blow to foreign prestige, not merely in Hong Kong but in every treaty-port, for you cannot do such things and keep your standing among the Chinese, whatever sentimentalists and missionaries may say. Now the officers of ships registered in Hong Kong have to take almost as many orders from their crews as they give.[5]

5   The seamen's strike of 1922 began in January with the grievances of the British territory's seamen and members of the General Industrial Federation of Chinese Seamen regarding pay and pay inequality between Chinese and non-Chinese merchant seamen. The strike spread rapidly to other sectors, effectively shutting Hong Kong down. As the first major industrial action in the colony it provoked the authorities to respond with emergency anti-strike legislation. Still, approximately 30,000 deck hands and stokers continued a 52-day strike meaning 167 steamers were moored up causing serious losses to shipping companies. And an additional

Compared with China proper Hong Kong gives the impression of wealth. Rich Chinese come and settle in safety here, even have themselves born here, getting their share of the rich juice of the trans-shipping trade, erecting modern department-stores that cut deeply into the British merchant's semi-monopoly, becoming such good Britishers that the king now and then "Sirs" one of them. For all this and its modernity, perhaps an account of it, there is the same old poverty as elsewhere; crowds struggling for a bare existence, coolies and beggars with naked legs – though even at Christmas one does not exactly suffer from bare feet in Hong Kong – are almost as conspicuous as anywhere in China proper. Women break stone and carry cruel loads; when the steamers from Canton and Macao and who knows how many other neighboring places have come in and tied up towards

---

50,000 Chinese office workers, cooks, bakers, rickshaw pullers, transport workers, and the Chinese staff of Government House joined the action, making it a general strike. The Shipowners' Committee wrote to the Governor in March with details of a settlement. The strikers appeared victorious. Wage rises of 15 to 30 per cent were promised, and restrictions on the seamen's union lifted, while imprisoned strikers were released. But the victory was only partial, the terms only somewhat adhered to by the Shipowners' Committee, and industrial action was to rumble on throughout the 1920s in Hong Kong and along the southern Chinese coast.

midnight, coolies wrap themselves in their dirty straw mats or rags and lie down to sleep on the bare wharves.

MACAO

Even if one is in no mood to gamble or take part in some of the other iniquities on which it lives, the traveler in China should not of course fail to visit Macao, the oldest and long the most important European treaty-port and foreign concession in China. Four hours on a comfortable steamer, morning or afternoon, carries him across the bay to it from Hong Kong; drinking, gambling, and vice-living places are always well supplied with good and frequent transportation. It almost takes one's breath to realize that the Portuguese got Macao away back in the Ming dynasty, just half a century before the Manchus with whom all other nations of the West had their troubles had come out of their shell up in the bleak northwest territory. It was more than three hundred years later that those upstart powers, England and the United States, came in. When the British "factories" were chased out of Canton they asked to share Macao with the Portuguese, but those haughty Lusitanians refused to have any dealings with the island of shopkeepers, and so the British started a rival trading-port on the then almost uninhabited island which the Chinese still call Hsiang Gang, "sweet waters," which to the rude ears of the sailors of those days sounded like "Hong Kong," and now Macao is a village by comparison. There are signs in the cemetery that it was once a business place of several races, but it has long since sunk to the unimportance of a gambling-den, the chief Monte Carlo of the China coast and the greatest, because the most visible and tangible, of the several bad examples set by the West to the Far East.

Physically it is attractive. Built on a rocky tongue of land along a bare and rocky coast, which ships go clear around, so that they skirt the wharfless Praya Grande first, it is just such a mixture of Portuguese and Chinese, with hints of other influences, as you would expect such a colony four centuries on the China coast to be.[6] The cobbled streets on which the hard-rubber-tired rickshaws bounce are so very different from those of China proper, for neither are those of Cintra and back-street Lisbon.[7] On the seaside of the town there is a pleasant promenade under shade-trees held up by the sea-wall upon which typhoons now and then wreak their vengeance. Frequently a Chinese

---

6   Praya (or alternatively Praia) Grande Bay, otherwise known as Nam Van and officially known as Ou Mun, is located on the east side of the Macau Peninsula, and traditionally served as the colony's chief promenade.

7   More commonly spelt Sintra, the resort town in the foothills of Portugal's Sintra Mountains, near Lisbon.

funeral, with certain modifications showing Portuguese influence, makes procession along this Praya Grande; in the cool of the evening important citizens and their legal or self-chosen spouses ride up and down it.

Two-story arcades run entirely around the waterfront; old medieval European houses in pink, red, blue, and other vivid colors stretch along hard European streets; old forts, ancient churches, the oldest lighthouse on the China coast, queer junks with khaki sails silhouetted against the sunset, a terrific smell of dried fish, are among the main features of the picture.[8] Shark's fins and all manner of *peixe salgado*, split and filled with salt by the men who catch them and forthwith sewed up by their women, hang and lie before scores of shops.[9] It is a hilly town, so that there are many fine seascapes for the climbing; Camões' Gardens with its small royal palms to emphasize Macao's relationship to Brazil, filled with huge tumbled boulders from among which spring these and other trees, the grotto where the great poet was wont to sit, faced now by a stone singing his praises in Portuguese and English, draw the visitor to one end of town, while near the other is a Chinese temple piled up a bouldered hillside, an ancient caravel carved

---

8   The lighthouse at the Guia Fortress was constructed between 1864 and 1865. The lighthouse is 91.4 metres (300 ft) tall and has a light visible for some 32 kilometres (20 miles).

9   *Peixe salgado* being salted fish of various types.

on a great stone in its lower compound, for the gods here are reputed to give special ear to the prayers of mariners and those about to go to sea.[10] Then there is the gateway between Macao and Chinese territory, under the constant vigilance of jet-black Portuguese soldiers, outside which in a temple a few *li* across the plain, toward the hills that loom in the distance beyond, Caleb Cushing and a son of Daniel Webster signed the first treaty between China and the United States. [11] Of all these things perhaps the most symbolical of Macao is the empty façade of an ancient church, left from the early days of pious Portugal, that stands on a hilltop like a skeleton of the past.[12]

---

10   Luís de Camões (1524-1580), Portugal's national poet best known for his epic poem *Os Lusíadas* (first published 1572), had been appointed to the rather macabre post of Superintendent for the Dead and Missing for Macau in 1562, serving de facto from 1563 until 1564 or 1565. Legend says he wrote part of *Os Lusíadas* in Macao.

11   The definition of a Chinese *li* has changed over the years but was at the time approximately a third of a mile. The 'hills' being those of Lapa (now flattened and renamed Wanzai). Caleb Cushing (1800-1879), as US Ambassador to China, signed the Treaty of Wangxia (Wanghia) in 1844 establishing US treaty rights in China. It was America's first formal treaty with China. Another American signatory was Daniel Fletcher Webster (1813-1862), American diplomat and son of veteran New Hampshire and Massachusetts congressman Daniel Webster (1782-1852).

12   The seventeenth-century ruins of Saint Paul's.

There is naturally a great mixture of races in Macao. Pretty white women with brown babies peer forth from gaily colored houses or come out for a ride when the sun is low; the five races of mankind may now and then be seen in a single countenance. Three hundred white Portuguese troops form the nucleus of the garrison; the rest are Mozambique negroes from another Portuguese colony.[13] Timorista soldiers from the Portuguese half of the island of Timor, much like the Dyaks of Borneo, once did duty here, but they could not stand the climate.[14] Then, too, a place of Macao's habits must have policemen, and they are of many kinds. Dark-brown Aryans from Goa, Chinese, Hindus and Sikhs, in turbans rather than helmets, mixed breeds of all these and more, including descendants of the Japanese Christians, a species of Oriental Huguenots,

---

13   Colonial soldiers originally from Portuguese East Africa were regularly stationed in Macao alongside Portuguese regulars. Around the time Franck visited the colony, there had been several partially successful uprisings against poor pay and bad conditions by white soldiers which led the Governor, Artur Tamagnini de Sousa Barbosa, to request that Lisbon send additional troops from Portuguese East Africa in an attempt to divide and conquer the rebellious troops stationed in Macao. The strategy largely worked.

14   The other (or western) half of Timor being controlled by the Dutch. Dyak is more commonly spelt Dayak now.

who fled here generations ago, patrol the streets in close succession.[15]

To the world at large Macao is synonymous with gambling. Lottery-tickets prominently marked with the name of the "Santa Casa de Misericórdia," that they may pretend even to themselves that they are devoted to the *beneficencia publica*, decorate the fronts of shops.[16]

By day Macao is languid, but with the coming of night bright lights bring out everywhere the narrow and cobbled, the crowded and noisy streets that are not very different from those of China proper, except that

---

15   Christian Japanese refugees from Nagasaki had fled from the religious persecution of the Tokugawa regime. Originally tolerated in Japan, their success at converting and recruiting came to be seen as a threat to the stability of the regime. Consequently in 1614 Christianity was outlawed. By the 1630s persecution of Japanese Christian converts had become intense and many were martyred – burned at the stake – forcing the survivors to flee. A number settled in Macao. Franck's comparison is to the Huguenots of the French Protestant Church who, somewhat later than the Japanese Christians, left France to escape persecution.

16   Santa Casa de Misericórdia is a Portuguese charity founded in 1498 whose mission is to treat and support the sick and the disabled, as well as abandoned newborns. The Santa Casa da Misericórdia (Holy House of Mercy) building, originally constructed in 1569, remains standing in Senado Square. It originally operated as a medical clinic, orphanage and refuge for widows of sailors lost at sea.

the gambling-houses and other "places of iniquity" are even more numerous than anywhere in China; the clack of wooden sandals, the clash of mah-jongg games, the screeching of sing-song girls in brilliantly lighted hotels and brothels – as in Brazil there is no distinct line of demarcation between the two – continue unabated until long after the mere sight-seeing visitor has taken to his bed. In one establishment is the famous gambling-wheel banished from Manila when it changed its nationality.[17] Scores if not hundreds of bright signs make the self-same announcement: "First Class Gambling House"; those not posing as first class occupy the intervening buildings and are little worse or better than their more pretentious rivals. All are three stories high, with coolies crowded about the long, mat-covered tables below, and upstairs, between the busy ground and the sleeping and living quarters of the inmates by day, with a railing about an opening in the floor to correspond to the table below, is the place where those of the better class, able to risk at least a Canton dollar at a time, sit on chairs and are cooled by electric fans.[18]

17 Roughly in 1898 after the United States took control of the Philippines following Spain's defeat in the Spanish-American War.

18 That is to say one Canton silver dollar.

Scrawny indoor types, some of the men in undershirts or stripped to the waist, with fingernails like cats' claws, many wearing jade or imitation bracelets, a few women of the less respectable class, all Chinese except here and there a queer-looking foreigner, lean from their chairs or stools over the railings. For all their bright lights the establishments are anything but palatial, rather decrepit, after the Chinese and Portuguese fashion, none too clean. Tea, toasted melon-seeds, shelled peanuts, sweets, a bit of fruit are set on the table-topped railing before each new arrival; downstairs, where even coppers are not scorned, the clients stand and have no refreshments. Pads of paper in ruled squares, the sheets tied together instead of being bound, pencils fastened with long strings to the railing, invite the gambler to begin his calculations. The table below is some twenty feet long, the money laid on the four sides of squares a foot each way in a dozen places along it by those who are trying their luck, between them trays full of money of the house – coppers, Canton twenty-cent pieces, silver dollars, bills of five and ten and even higher. While the bets are being placed the croupier at the end of the table sits smoking with the bored but otherwise expressionless face of his kind the world over. A heap of polished brass "cash" lies before him, half covered with a brass disk with a handle; Chinese fan-tan habitués become so expert that they have been known to count correctly a whole heap of such counters before the bets are closed. At length the croupier picks up a thin wand, and with the exact motions of an experienced surgeon pulls the now uncovered "cash" toward him, four at a time, with the extreme end of the rod. The number left at the end of the counting wins.

Some croupiers are said to be so clever that they can keep one "cash" hidden under another as they draw them in and thus change the count in favor of the house. Half a dozen men behind the trays, all in the last stages of boredom, pay out money to the winners with the easy speed of experts. Some goes into the little baskets on the ends of strings in which other bored Celestials, the same who served the tea and squash-seeds, let down bets from the floor of the élite above, with a monotonous singsong *"Yat man sam chalk,"* as nearly as my ear caught their Cantonese dialect – "One dollar on No. 3." Winners seemed to forfeit a copper for each twenty-cent piece won, as a kind of tax to the Government or to the house. All night long year in and year out this goes on in dozens of establishments in every down-town street. It is as stupid a game as could well be imagined, calling for no other mental effort than patience and guessing. Ah, well, life is a gamble anyway. But this is so fatuous a way to lose, or even to get, money.

Graft reigns supreme in Macao. Everyone squeezes, down to the police patrolling the cobbled streets. Gambling, opium, prostitution are the only reasons for its existence. Portuguese government officials with salaries of a hundred "Mex" dollars a month have big, luxurious houses, a dozen servants, expensive automobiles, mistresses in silks and jewels.[19] It is the only Portuguese colony, they say, that pays dividends. Its officials not long ago arranged with the politicians at home to let them spend six million on a breakwater that is not needed, there being no trade worth mentioning, and which will probably never be finished; in other words they want the income to stay in Macao, or go into their own pockets, instead of being spent in the Metropole or in the other colonies. Macao officials more or less secretly encourage the Chinese pirates who infest this coast to come here and spend their winnings in gambling, smoking opium, entertaining the ladies, and probably outfitting for new

---

19 The eagle-headed Mexican dollar, aka the "Dollar Mex", was frequently used by foreigners in China and Macao. According to the American journalist and advertising guru Carl Crow, who spent the interwar years in China, the Dollar Mex was introduced 'to avoid carrying around five-to-ten-pound lumps of silver *(taels)* as spending money….prices at hotels and stores are quoted in them.' The value of the Dollar Mex varied in the 1920s and 1930s from slightly more than a US silver dollar to about 50 per cent of the US dollar's value.

expeditions. A missionary whose work among lepers of the coast makes it impossible for him to denounce them meets dozens of pirates in its streets, usually dressed like middle-class merchants; many a big hotel blazes and roars with the festivities by which the sea-rovers make up for the perils and hardships of their calling.[20]

---

20   The Portuguese established a leprosarium on the island of Dom João (now Xiao, or Little, Hengqin) which required a platoon of troops stationed on the island to protect the colony from pirates. Macau had a number of leprosariums – in the 1740s the King of Portugal, Dom João V, had ordered that serious steps be taken to study and contain leprosy in Portugal's overseas colonies.

ROVING THROUGH SOUTHERN CHINA
(II)

A SHORT WINTER IN THE "SOUTHERN CAPITAL"[21]

APPROACHING CANTON

I came to Canton from all four points of the compass during my last year in China. The first time was by the comfortable and familiar way of tourists and businessmen – steamer from Hong Kong. There are several boats by day and as many by night, the fares double on the somewhat more palatial, with the added privilege of being under the protection, whatever it may amount to in present-day

---

21   At this time the new republican government of China was split between the various warlord-controlled government in Northern China and based in Peking (Beijing) and the so-called "Southern Government" led by Sun Yat-sen and with its capital in Canton.

China, of the British flag. By day one slips across the blue bay of Hong Kong, dotted with islands in the offing, and into what turns out to be a river, though at first it looks like more bay, tawny hills gashed and split by torrential rains gradually infolding it, long arms of sea-blue water reaching far into the valleys. Soon the hills are lower, and presently they are gone.

The delta country widens to a fertile plain, one of the richest in the world, that spreads out for mile after mile on either hand. Long ditches intersect broad stretches of olive-green rice, willows lean along the watercourses, bamboos and banana-plants fringe the mud-walled villages that are rarely out of sight of one another, so intensely is this district cultivated. The river is not always easy navigating, one gathers from the sight of a big steamer, under a British captain of decades of experience on this run, breaking in two where it was driven ashore in a narrow part of it. Whampoa and the two pagodas on Honam Island at length appear in succession, a clump of hills known as White Cloud Mountain rises off the starboard bow, and before the sun is far on its decline an almost Occidental sky-line grows up along the banks of the now crowded river and one has reached Canton, its modernized face masking the ancient city behind.[22]

---

22 Whampoa Island, once the chief anchorage for foreign ships engaged in the China Trade, is now known as Pazhou

Perhaps the more popular way is to leave Hong Kong toward the end of the theater-hour and, after watching the play of the moonlight across the sea and its islands and the coast that eventually shuts it in, to be awakened by a mighty hubbub and find the steamer warping its way into one of several wharves flanking a Bund already in an uproar of chaotic noises even at this unearthly hour.[23] Quite as crowded is the Chu-kiang, the Pearl River, as the Cantonese miscall their main stream, boats of every size and description dotting it as far as the eye can see, whole streets of house-boats in the real sense of the word running out at right angles from the overpopulated shore, craft so thick that every time a steamer docks several floating houses all but get crushed, or their families all but cut in two by hawsers; yet though there is much shrieking and futile paddling, they never seem to come completely to grief, or keep out of the way the next time.

Island, a subdistrict of Haizhu in Guangzhou. Honam (sometimes Henan) Island ("South of the River") is similarly part of Haizhu now and was close to the site of the former foreign "factories" (trading warehouses) where the foreigners were permitted to live and trade in season. White Cloud Mountain is now known as Baiyun Mountain, a few miles to the north of Guangzhou.

23   The term "bund" is borrowed from Hindi and originally referred to a dyke or raised embankment alongside a stretch of water.

"Next to the exuberance of the population," as some traveler of long ago well put it, "the number of boats employed on the rivers of southern China is the most striking circumstance belonging to the Chinese Empire." Many thousands of the citizens of Canton are born and die on boats, are married on them, and buried from them; they form almost a race apart, more aggressive, more independent, than those who have to cringe for life ashore. It might be a way to overcome our own "housing crisis" to have a few millions of our people take to living on the water. The family altar occupies the center and best part of almost every boat, and this part is often surprisingly clean, if the water of the Chu-kiang can really cleanse anything. The same question as to how the boat-dwellers earn a living confronts the beholder here and in Foochow and elsewhere.[24] The men, and boys old enough to compete in the chaotic Cantonese struggle for existence, are often away pulling rickshaws or doing other work ashore, so that it is usually the women, the younger children helping, who stand at the stern twisting back and forth the big oar tied to the deck with a rope of native fibers with which they scull passengers or cargo in their floating homes along the river or through the channels, too narrow for rowing. If the man is at home he commonly sits at the prow, giving orders, now and

_____

24   Foochow = Fuzhou.

then using a bamboo pole, and collecting any money due. Thus the women of the vast water-dwelling population of Canton are quite as expert with the oar as are their offspring at sleeping on their backs while they scull. A duck does not swim more casually than they handle their boats.

Up some of the dirty creeks that divide the city there are toll-bridges of an old plank laid from boat to boat, or an aged craft itself serving as a bridge, the women and children of the family clearing the way whenever a boat comes up or down the stream and expecting a few "cash" for all who walk across it. There are whole streets of "slipper-boats," of cargo-craft ever ready for any job that offers, and filled with all the intimate sights of a household, all manner of queer junks of every size, that wander away up country now and then and some day wander back again, all kinds of strange imitations of gunboats flying the flag – by design or some amusing coincidence bearing a flaming sun – of the Government of Sun Yat-sen. Junks with high and curiously painted poops, some carrying cannon of two centuries ago against the pirates, are anchored out in the river, or arrive or depart so deeply loaded that one wonders they can float. Municipal ferries in the shape of miserable rowboats ply back and forth across the river to an equally crowded section of the city on Honam Island at a few "cash" a passenger – if he happens to have them;

big sternwheelers run by no other engine than a dozen or score of coolies marching a treadmill inside jostle coasting-vessels and foreign steamers flying many flags, from British to Portuguese, with their Sikh guards and futile guard-cages.[25]

Whole streets of "flower-boats," in which ladies of the most ancient of female professions entertain, mainly by night, the male population of Canton, stretch their gaudy way along the river, particularly before that section of town that became our home. In the morning, not too early, you will find the girls combing and prinking, repainting their sadly impaired façades, while slatternly old mother busies herself with the housework, redecorates the family altar, and refreshes the place for the night's customers. These women of the "flower-boats" face life with a cheerful demeanor, as if, true fatalists, they are not going to be any

---

25   Franck notes the Sikh guards and guard-cages (into which passengers were to retreat and lock themselves in the event of pirate attack). They were both relatively new innovations on the coastal steamers between Hong Kong and Canton following the post-World War I advent of the so-called "Passenger Ploy". This involved male and female pirates posing as passengers and then attempting to take control of the ship. The hijackings were often violent and resulted in pirate, crew, and passenger deaths. Subsequently, Hong Kong's 1914 Piracy Ordinances were updated in 1922 to include the legal requirement to employ additional guards (overwhelmingly Sikhs were recruited) and to install safety cages.

more miserable than necessary over the lot to which the gods have assigned them.

Perhaps it is because it turns to the river its most Westernized front that Canton gives the impression at once of being engaged in an enormous amount of building, more modern building than any other Chinese city, outside the foreign concessions.[26] For a mile or more along the river-front boulevard stretches a long row of five- and six-story structures, culminating in the great Sun department store.[27] Not, as many tourists conclude, and buy souvenirs for the folks at home accordingly, owned, but merely mulcted, by Sun Yat-sen – rising above all else to a tower so high that it not only charges but actually collects a fee from those who wish to go up and look out over Canton and its vicinity.[28] Shrieks, shouts, and

---

26   Franck is here thinking primarily of the Shanghai, Wuhan and Tientsin (Tianjin) treaty ports, all with waterfront bunds.

27   The 12-storey Da (or 'Big') Sun building was erected between 1918 and 1922 by Chong Choy, from Xiangshan (a city renamed Zhongshan after Sun Yat-sen, known in China as Sun Zhongshan in 1925) who had made money in Sydney in the 1890s. Sun was a chain, beginning with a store on Hong Kong's Des Voeux Road that opened in 1912. The Canton store had four elevators and its own power generators.

28   Mulcted – to defraud, especially of money: to swindle (Merriam-Webster). It seems Franck believed Sun was extracting money by charging visitors to go to the viewing platforms on the top floor.

chaos are constant in this river of screaming pullers of rattling, buggy-wheeled rickshaws, carriers of heavy pole-borne burdens, peddlers, beggars, boatmen – more often women, quite as sturdy and capable in the struggle for existence – clamoring for passengers, ungreased autobuses constantly snorting to and from Tung Shan[29], dreadful things with atrocious wooden seats in no way suited to a foreigner's sitting posture, jolting and jumping beneath their inexpert chauffeurs, causing few deaths only by miracle.

Official automobiles with one weak-faced man of importance lolling inside and four, six, even eight soldiers in khaki on the running boards, cocked rifle-handled automatics in hand, dash up to the Asia Hotel, follow close about the simple youth in flannel as he makes his way to the elevator, and descend with him to climb again all over the car as it leaves. [30] Canton is peculiarly given

---

29 Tung Shan is now part of the Dongshankou area of Guangzhou, a generally well-heeled suburb in Yuexiu District that was in the process of being developed at the time. It is now a rare example of a district of well-preserved architecture of residential mansions and villas as well as various Western-style buildings including the Tung Shan Christian Church (Baptist).

30 Franck is looking at the C96 produced by the German arms manufacturer Mauser at the time. Bootleg copies of the automatic were manufactured in China (known as the

to this parading with cocked automatics in hand. Swarms of pedestrians pour in and out of the narrow streets and along the Bund itself, with a mingling of uniformed employees of the big stone custom-house and the post-office, perhaps even an eccentric foreigner willing to walk the hundred yards from the foreign concession to the steamer wharves, haughty with his efforts to appear effortless in all this maelstrom, all the rank and file and chaos of Chinese life stretching as far as the eye can see and farther than the ears can hear or the nose protest down the wide street between the more or less foreign face of the city and the river with its even more crowded streets of boats.

The only semi-calm in all the scene is a small island close off the Bund, known as Dutch Folly, because it was once offered to Holland as a concession by the Chinese, who thought it worth nothing, an erroneous impression in which the slow-thinking Dutchmen agreed with them. Wu Ting-fang once had his home and office in the rambling fort now overrun by soldiers, like every other available space in town, that covers all the western end of

---

"box cannon", or in Shanghai the "Red 9") in the first half of the twentieth century, often with the addition of a wooden detachable shoulder stock, a feature unique to the automatic in China.

the island,[31] overhanging the river and shaded by two big banian-trees; and at the farther end a Chinese admiral in bronze and full Western regalia stands gazing off down the river. The original, it seems, was assassinated at a feast to which a rival had invited him, and with one of those delicate touches peculiar to the Celestial character the assassin provided the statue in memory of his victim. Since they are otherwise so rarely called to account, it would seem only just that our own assassins, if some means could be found to raise them to the Chinese standard, should have the courtesy to make some such reparation. Though the harbor-master advised against it, the island was soon to be connected with the mainland, so

---

31 The Dutch Folly fort was a specific type of fort built in shallow water, near the shore, in the second half of the nineteenth century. Usually exclusively for military defence with no intention of being used as normal living quarters, though it appears Wu Ting-fang did occupy it for some years when in the service of Sun Yat-sen's Southern Government. The Dutch Folly at Canton had a several-storey coned tower. The fort was demolished when land reclamation ended its island status. Malacca-born Wu Ting-fang (1842-1922) was a Chinese diplomat, lawyer (admitted as a barrister in Hong Kong and unofficial member of the Legislative Council), politician and writer who served as Minister of Foreign Affairs (1921-1922) and briefly as Acting Premier (May-June 1917) during the early years of the Chinese Republic. Franck would have been aware of Wu perhaps due to his having been the Qing's ambassador to the United States between 1908-1909.

that some of the money which the Southern party seems to need even more constantly than the other dictators of China could be raised by selling it.

Down the river where those take sampans who miss the launch to the Canton Christian College on its few self-conveniencing trips, the Bund peters out in blocks of four-story buildings once devoted to ladies of the allegedly easy life, but now the noisome and sheveled unpaid dwellings of mercenary soldiers and other discordant elements.[32] Time was when you could descend at the station, over the bridge beyond, just four hours after boarding an express at Kowloon, the Hong Kong mainland; but though tourist bureaus still hopefully advertise the advantages of this route, years have passed since the civil wars in Kwangtung Province closed it to through traffic.[33]

The newly arrived foreigner is more likely to go the other way along the swarming Bund, toward a glimpse of trees, and find himself wondering a few yards beyond the steamer wharves what all the semi-forest and grassy lawns and general un-Chinese order and cleanliness before him mean. Then he realizes, as he crosses a brief gated bridge guarded at the Bund end by an Oriental in French uniform, who lets him enter with almost a

32 Sheveled is a now out-of-date way of saying "disheveled".
33 Franck is referring to the Kowloon-Canton Railway (KCR). Kwangtung is Guangdong.

welcoming smirk, though he scrutinizes all the slender stream of his fellow-Easterners who pass the gate, that he is on Shameen.[34]

SHAMEEN ISLAND

Though the Portuguese were the first Europeans, Marco Polo and no doubt a few less articulate of his kind excepted, to come into contact with Chinese, Canton became a treaty port, which was soon to wipe out Macao's more than three centuries of advantage, long before Amoy, Foochow, Ningpo, and Shanghai followed suit or Hong Kong raised the British flag.[35] Some decades later the Canton "factories" – for which read trading-posts – of the English and French were robbed and ruined, and several traders killed, whereupon the two governments informed the Manchu dynasty at Peking that they must have a spot of their own where they could rule and protect their own people. "Very well," replied the Manchus, their tongues in their cheeks as usual in dealing with crude outside barbarians, "you may have Shameen." Sandy Face was the

34   Shameen Island, the foreign concession of Canton. More commonly now called Shamian.

35   Amoy, Foochow and Ningpo = Xiamen, Fuzhou and Ningbo.

patch of sand a bit up the river from the Dutch Folly, below water at high tide, and one of the principal garbage-heaps of the unspeakable Chinese city behind it.[36] To the surprise of the Chinese the mad foreigners accepted the offer, spent what was a lot of money in those days to fill in between the stone embankment with which they encircled it, and proceeded to build a foreign settlement on the resulting forty-four acres, as annual rental for which they pay to this day a few strings of "cash" per *mou*.[37]

Now three broad streets shaded by venerable old trees run the length of the oblong island, with cross streets in proportion, two on the river-front and the back canal respectively, the one down the center of the island so wide that tennis-courts stretch between the two sidewalks. Along these leisurely streets suggestive of an unspoiled New England village are the foreign banks, consulates, the ancient establishment that still boasts itself the only foreign hotel in Canton, nearly all the old foreign business houses, and mainly in the upper stories of these, many of the foreign residences.[38]

---

36   Shameen literally means "sandy surface" or "face" in Chinese.

37   *Mou* = a Chinese unit of land measurement that varies with location, but is commonly 806.65 square yards (0.165 acre, or 666.5 square metres).

38   The Victoria Hotel.

Perhaps the first and abiding impression, at least to one fresh from the interior of China, is the prettiness of the miniature foreign city on an island hardly big enough for a racetrack. Its spreading trees and bright flower-beds, the lawns that stretch continuously between the dignified rows of houses, its trim cleanliness, its spacious calm for all its small size, so that precious as is every acre it still maintains a large football-field before the landing-stage, make as great a contrast between this handful of foreign soil and the city from which only a narrow creek far-famed for its smells separates it as the contrast between Europe and China. Only two little gated bridges connect it with Canton – with China, one is almost betrayed into putting it – and these close by night; no Chinese boats may moor to the Shameen side of the narrow canal dividing this little alien world from the Orient, though they crowd in serried ranks, like automobiles nose to curb in a prairie town on a Saturday night, along every inch of the Canton side twenty feet away.

It seems ridiculous to associate thoughts of business with so pretty, so toy-like a place, and it is not hard to get those who play at it to quit their ledgers and codes and come out and frankly play. Here is a little of the surge and blare of Shanghai; one fancies Western business life was much like this in those far-off days when this bit of sand was turned over to the despised barbarians. Here are no automobiles, not even the rattle of wagons; not so much as a rickshaw can pass the vigilant Cerberus who guards either of the two entrances across the Stinks – though to be sure two or three foreigners seem to have a "special pull" with the municipal council or whatever governing body Shameen boasts; [39] the West itself, to say nothing of the East, would seem strange without its specially privileged – and there is no traffic more terrifying than baby-carriages and a few bicycles, once in a great while a chair for some aged resident whose pedestrian days are over.

One fifth of the island belongs to the French and the rest is British, so that the Gallic architecture and atmosphere of the few acres at the eastern entrance change several times before they terminate in Japanese at the western end, where the Japanese have taken advantage of their British ally. Perhaps, like other Western concessions in China, Shameen has more Chinese than foreign residents; not, however, as householders. In Canton things are the other way about; it is the foreigners who must seek

---

39   Here Franck is making a play on words. Cerberus, in Greek mythology, is the multi-headed dog that guards the gates to the underworld (Hades) to prevent the dead from leaving. Cerberus also guards the Temple of Styx, the fourth and final area in Hades. Franck replaces Styx with "Stinks", reiterating the malodorous nature of the canal separating Shameen from Canton proper.

refuge among the Chinese. Shameen is too small even for new-comers of our own race to find housing upon it, so that it resembles those aristocratic sections of our cities where the old families whose forebears guessed well in their land-buying have everything within their grasp. The likeness might be continued, to mention certain village weaknesses of human nature, somewhat different from the city weaknesses of Shanghai, for as a resident put it, "There can't be any gossip or scandal on Shameen, because we all live in one another's pockets and know one another's history from the day we or our ancestors landed in China."

No Chinese except house-servants are allowed to live on the island, but every office has its Chinese clerks, and every foreign household, be its head only a lone bachelor, has its cluster of Chinese domestics; thousands of other Celestials find some excuse to enter Shameen, some merely to report the wonders of the foreigners' ways of living to their open-mouthed villages; not a few, though it is against the rules, make the broad cement sidewalks between the two gates a thoroughfare from one part of Canton proper to another, so that if the streets of Sandy Face were not so amply wide and so many for the size of

The cash register of Canton, where silver 20-cent pieces are the largest money, consists of a board with depressions in it into which coins are shaken

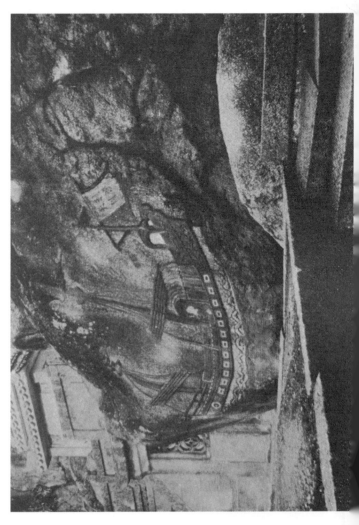

On a huge boulder in the compound of a Chinese temple in Macao, where mariners and those about to go to sea come to offer rewards for their safety, is carved an ancient caravel

Looking across Portuguese Macao

Lei Fuk-lum, ex-bandit boss of Honam Island, lives in a feudal castle with moat drawbridge and rifle loopholes for his many armed defenders

From the last bridge on the labyrinthine way to our Canton home in the western suburb stretched a Venetian scene that was a little more pleasant at high than low tide

In Canton and its adjoining districts, tower-like pawnshop-warehouses bulking high above other buildings offer protection to valuables in frequent times of danger

*Along the waterfront of Canton, crowded streets of house-boats
stretch for miles*

In Canton, where thieves are legion and heat often intense, sliding doors of stout poles protect most well-to-do households and shops

the little island, the mere foreigner would be constantly jostled as along the mountain roads of Kuling.[40]

To-day by no means all the foreign residents of Canton live, or even do business, on Shameen. As with the Legation Quarter at Peking, the fiction is kept up that all those except the missionaries do so, but in practice you will find them scattered in half a dozen large communities, and as many small ones, to the east and to the west, up and down across the river, and across it again from the populous island of Honam to the mainland beyond.

CANTON

Few of the treaty-ports and important cities of China are known to the outside world by a name that would mean anything to the Chinese who live in them. "Canton" is derived from the English transliteration – a politer word for mispronunciation, slurring, indolence of ear and tongue – of Kwangtung, the province of which it is the capital. To the Chinese, Canton city is Kwangchowfu, and it has been a Chinese city only since 1053 A.D., when the Tai race, which long inhabited this southern part of what

---

40   Kuling (now Guling), the summer resort on Lu Mountain in Jiujiang, Jiangxi province, much favoured by foreigners and founded by missionaries.

is now, but was not then, China proper was driven out in a series of battles and dispersed among the mountains to the southwest, where we know it today as Shan or Laos. The people of other provinces insist that the Cantonese still belong to another race, but that is little more than an intentional slur. The women of Kwangtung Province do not bind their feet – and consequently do coolie labor almost equally with the men – partly because of the influence of the remnants of the tribes that once reigned along this coast. The boat-people are said to be remnants of those tribes and never to have bound their feet. The real Chinese of Kwangtung kept the practice until only a generation ago – even the mother of Sun Yat-sen had "lily feet" – and as it is now almost unknown in that province perhaps there is hope that the whole country will emancipate its women to that extent in another century.[41]

---

41 Following the growth of anti-foot binding societies in the nineteenth century, in 1912 the new republican government officially banned foot binding, though the ban was not actively implemented. It was reiterated by the progressive May 4th Movement in 1919 who saw binding as a sign of China's "backwardness". Though implementation was patchy, and some provinces and regions outlawed the practice faster and more effectively than others, it's fair to say Franck was overly pessimistic in his assessment that it would not be successfully ended as a practice in the twentieth century.

Canton to-day is just as Chinese as Peking, though the two great cities do not talk the same language, and many of the details of life are quite different. Canton food is not Peking food, even though melon-seeds and peanuts, "gambaying" and hot towels, are as common to one as to the other; nor for that matter are the "chow mein" and "chop suey" of our own Chinese restaurants known to either of them.[42] Where Peking has but four tones for the 420 monosyllabic sounds that are said to make up its language, and manages to talk well, nay, at times too much, on any subject, Canton has nine, and it behooves the man who would speak Cantonese and not make embarrassing mistakes to know them. We knew one American, many years a resident at Canton, who went to a mandarin-speaking part of the country and, mixing his tones in trying to say what we without imperfect alphabet can only spell as *feng hsing*, meaning "take these letters to the post," caused his coolie to go out and hire help to bring him instead a church organ, called "wind-box." I well remember soon after our arrival in China how a Cantonese doctor in Peking raised his hands in helplessness at my request that he tell my rickshaw-man to come back at six o'clock. At least twice during my Chinese wanderings I acted as interpreter between two

---

42   *Ganbei* (干杯), literally "dry cup", or to drink a toast in Mandarin Chinese.

Chinese, one of them a Cantonese speaking English but no mandarin. It was not unlike the case of the Russian I ran across in an interior town, who looked enough like me to have passed for a brother, yet with whom I could not exchange a word except in the language of the astonished Chinese about us. My own experience was that it is easier in Canton to find someone speaking English than the mandarin tongue of most of the country. But Canton and Peking – Indo-China and Korea for that matter – use the same written characters, so that China's civilisation, which undoubtedly is the same civilisation from northern Manchuria to Hainan, has as its chief vehicle of unity not speech but the written language.[43]

We once saw in Peking a motion-picture the first scenes of which were in China, and we concluded that it was either many years old or had been done in a Los Angeles Canton. For the rickshaws were clumsy, ugly things with wooden buggy-tires, and moved so slowly and ponderously that we could barely recognize in them the very early ancestors of the handsome wire-wheeled, pneumatic-tired vehicles in which we were wafted as noiselessly and smoothly as on a magic carpet across the capital of Kublai Khan, and other cities of the North. But when we reached Canton we found that the movie

43   Franck's assertion of Korea and Indochina using Chinese characters is of course incorrect.

was right. Somehow we had expected greater rather than less progress in the South. In some ways it is more progressive and up to date, but not in its ordinary means of conveyance. There were those very rickshaws we had sneered at on the screen, their lumbering buggy-wheels rattling and jolting on their crude axles, the hard tires that made a ride as painful as in a Peking-cart registering every hole in the wide but broken surfaces of the new streets, feeling every rut or pebble like a foot in a soleless shoe, so slow that probably, if one came to figure it out, the slowness of life in Canton in spite of its incessant hubbub and apparent rush is due to the languor of the Canton rickshaw-man, who moves like a horse-carriage compared to the automobile swiftness of the runners of the North.

Moreover he is decidedly more expensive, even on the basis of mileage. Here you did not "talk price" for your transportation; there were fixed rates by zones, and no arguing at the end of the run. The cost of a rickshaw ride was several times more than in Peking, where most Canton prices would have seemed extravagant, and no doubt more nearly fair to the coolie. Yet in the end he was no better off than his Peking contemporary. Exorbitant taxes, the curse of Canton, were assessed against each runner as well as against the rickshaw monopoly owning almost all the vehicles catering to the general public. The runner paid seventy cents a day for his rickshaw; he was forced to pay graft to a head runner, to a type of labor-union, taxes for this, that, and the other, and seldom earned an average of a dollar and a half a day in depreciated Canton currency.

The Canton police are less gentle with the rickshaw men than are those of New York towards its taxicab drivers. Two rickshaw men fall to fighting over their place in the long line shrieking at the wharves or the entrance to Shameen for the few fares in sight. It is not, of course, a fist-fight after the fashion in the West; the East does not "double its hands" and strike. Instead there is some slapping and much screaming. A policeman steps up, flails both men across the backs with the kind of riding-crop that takes the place of a billy in Canton, and then snatches a cushion out of each vehicle. It might not work on Broadway, even with automobile cushions, but in the East it saves argument and is an effective form of bail, for if the men do not come to the police-station and pay their fine the cushions will go as squeeze to someone. So no doubt the guardians of such law and order as exist in Canton are only too glad when this indirect summons is not obeyed.

***

If one's way lies by water, as it so often does in Canton, a boat is the obvious answer. Boatmen, or women, work more cheaply, if still not anything like their fellows in the North. Or if one lives out at Tung Shan – "East Mountain," a mere knoll about which are scattered many foreign houses, mission schools, a cluster of residences of the higher employees of what is now only in name the railway to Kowloon – one can trust himself to a frequent Ford bus, though that also will not be inexpensive.[44] If one is wealthy, or employed by a wealthy foreign corporation, or the representative of a foreign government, naturally a private motor-boat or automobile solves the problem. Otherwise one might better walk, for though sedan-chairs can be had from their *hongs*, mere dens opening on many of the narrow streets, in which the men lie smoking opium while one of their number watches for fares, they are not merely costly but their carriers often drowsy with their drug and independent to the point of insolence.

I could walk from the home we had in the western suburb out to Tung Shan at the other end of town in an hour; that is, the distance of a short five-to-ten-cent trolley ride in any American city. Yet to take the available Canton forms of transportation, two or three different kinds for the trip, cost a Canton dollar, besides the tip that must be paid if you are to avoid a hubbub at your gate, or that of

---

44 Tung Shan being better known as Dongshan District, noted for the number of educational establishments located there. Dongshan was merged with Yuexiu District in 2005.

the man you have gone to visit, that will advertise your penuriousness to all the neighborhood; and by the time all is paid you will find that almost an hour has elapsed. But then, they say that our own Manila, not so far south of Canton, has no chairs, no boats, no rickshaws, hardly a carriage, and that no one will take an automobile out of a garage for less than five pesos.[45] Life in the Orient is by no means so inexpensive as the ludicrous wages of many Orientals would lead the inexperienced to believe.

***

Anachronism that they seem to us of the West, and even to some modern military commanders of China, the ancient city walls of that land have not only in most cases been left intact, but in almost any city of pride they have been kept as much in repair as the Chinese commonly keep anything, with the possible exception of the graves of their ancestors. There is a certain amount of superstition, too, and of course habit, connected with them; on my long trip through northwestern China the year before I had seen not a few city walls being almost rebuilt as protection against bandits, soldiery, unruly neighbors,

---

45   The Philippines in 1925 being under American control.

and evil spirits.[46] But the famous old city walls – the plural is justified – of Canton are gone.

Unlike almost every other city in "republican" China the "southern capital" has seen all but a corner of its once great barriers converted into boulevards, and even that last corner coolies of both sexes were carrying away, brick by blue-gray brick. It had been one of the most imposing walls in China, mentioned in every account of old Canton – twenty-five feet high, with seventeen gates, and, as the silt built up the bank of the river, a "new city" centuries old had also its separate wall. Since the story is current that Sun Yat-sen once, during his early days of plotting, escaped the Manchu beheader by getting over the city wall in disguise under the very noses of the Manchu soldiers, no doubt he took keen pleasure in demolishing it.

Now boulevards run wherever the walls ran before, and in other places as well, so that the old Canton to-day is Saikwan, the western suburb, which was once the newest.[47] As in so many other Chinese cities the best parts of town had gradually come to be outside the walls; now with the wide new streets the best buildings are growing

---

46   See Harry A Franck, *Wandering in Northern China* (New York: The Century Company, 1923).

47   Saikwan = Xiguan, an ancient town and an area in the Liwan district of Guangzhou located west of the old walled city adjacent to Shameen Island.

up again within the once walled city. The boulevards were cut through ruthlessly, the military marking their future course and tearing down, or forcing the owners themselves to tear down, anything that stood in their way, and those who had any land left might build again or decamp, as their desires or their financial condition dictated. At most, written promises someday to pay the owners, or squatters, were given, and neither the givers nor the receivers supposed for a moment that they would ever be kept. The mayor himself, son of the "great reformer" then still heading the "Southern Government," admitted that the promises were worthless.[48]

It is a rough way, this Chinese method, but perhaps it is the only one in a country where public spirit is at a low ebb, and where negotiations have a way of running on forever. The big streets left flatiron-shaped bits of houses, narrow shells of buildings, mere stairways to buildings now little more than second stories hanging out over the sidewalks. I suppose it is this furore of "improvement" and modernization that has left Canton with a single

---

48   Franck is here referring to Sun Fo (1891-1973), son of Sun Yat-sen, educated at University of California, Berkeley, and Columbia. He returned to China and was appointed Mayor of Canton, serving from 1920 to 1922 and again from 1923 to 1925.

p'ai-lou or memorial arch over its streets, for their absence seems strange in a great Chinese city.[49]

They are not exactly paved in asphalt, these new streets of Canton. They are dusty, and they are too wide, perhaps, for a place where the sun blazes down unpleasantly most of the months of the year. Their *ma-lu* (horse roads), as the Chinese miscall them, for nothing is so rare as a horse in Canton, may be progress, but it was more pleasant even in the milder sunshine of January to branch off from these broad, hot, dusty, ill-copied boulevards, honking with Fords and disagreeable with other nuisances, and wander away through the narrow old side streets, paved with big slabs of stone worn glass-smooth by millions of soft-shod feet, roofed over with oyster-shell awnings, the streets of old Canton, universal before this Sunny rage for copying the West struck it.[50] The Chinese are inordinately clever at building both their houses and their towns so as to keep out the sunshine where it is too keen.

---

49 More commonly *pailou*, a traditional style of Chinese architectural arch or gateway.

50 *Ma-lu* was a traditional word used in the late nineteenth century in Shanghai and then in the twentieth century in other Chinese cities to describe the larger roads being constructed – passable by horses or vehicles. Sometimes in Mandarin the phrase *Da Ma Lu* (big horse road) or 'main road' is used and sometimes in southern China, *Toa Beh Lo* in Hokkien.

The sunless old streets of Canton, across which the wide new ones cut like furrows across a hundred mole-holes, are dirty, of course, but unless they are swarming with the bumping traffic of rickshaws they are not otherwise unpleasant, for here is still the shaded life of the once walled city, where one can look back into the cool, always fascinating depths of a thousand homes, of all manner of ancient shops and businesses, that have changed but little since the days of Confucius. Besides, China does not seem China unless you are breasting a howling, jostling mob like a racing mountain stream of humanity, beneath an endless vista of gaudy upright gilded shop-signs; and once you are out on the wide *ma-lu* again where everyone has room and there is no excuse to jostle and to shout, where that crowdedness that is the very symbol of China almost disappears, life seems sluggish, anemic, no longer well worthwhile.

***

Shameen having no accommodations for us, we took an apartment – I mean it in quite the modern sense – out on the western edge of Saikwan, the western suburb. The municipal authorities of the "Southern capital" had announced their intention of inflicting this also with wide streets, as they had the walled city of which it was the chief overflow, and on paper six broad *ma-lu* already criss-crossed it; but it was our good luck to reach Canton and get away again right before this happened, just as we had antedated by a fraction the street-cars which I have no doubt have now ruined Peking entirely.[51] Saikwan was not an easy place to cross for those who do not like the transportation system nature gave them. At certain varying hours one could take a small boat from Shameen out through the "flower-boats" and all manner of human life and traffic, a smelly way under several low bridges, with now and then a bucket of slop thrown down as you passed from the houses falling sheer into the canal on either side, not from design to be sure, yet unpleasant for all that. Some of the boat-dwelling children were tied with ropes; others had a joint of bamboo on their backs as a life-preserver.

Except when the tide was high, which it rarely was when one needed or cared to travel, one could either take an unclean sedan chair, or walk. The narrow, ancient-China streets of unmodernised Saikwan were impossible even for rickshaws. To step across the British bridge at Shameen

---

51 Street-cars (or trams) were introduced into Peking in 1924 on several main thoroughfares along Chang'an Boulevard and around Chienmen (Qianmen). In the early years of their use there were complaints about their ungreased wheels making horrendous noises in what had been a relatively quiet city while rickshaw pullers complained about both the danger of getting caught in the tracks and the lost business to public transport.

and dive into the labyrinth of strangulated passageways that covered the big west suburb as with a net was to drop from the present, or at least from the nineteenth century, into the China of Marco Polo. Our way led past a bamboo Eiffel Tower from which the police watched for fires and other troubles, across a bridge where not a drop of water was seen in all the months we lived there, though one boat sat imbedded in the earth beside it, its family still living there serenely, across other bridges, a few steps long, with humped backs, that lifted us over the noisome canals up which we could float at high water, now with grounded boats loaded with wood and rice and the like, and rampant with the stench of low water.

It was a maze of streets through which a stranger could not have found his way with his life depending upon it, yet which we came to thread day or night as easily as a blind man finds his way by instinct. Here the old-style streets paved with immense slabs of stone, smooth as glass, were further constricted by the tables and wares of street-venders, that ubiquitous, raucous, tireless gentry, here and there by a street idol, on an already too narrow corner, where the masses stopped to burn much joss in the vain hope of better luck. Peep-hole shows, makers of magic, all manner of copper-catching schemes and contrivances lined the way, especially during festival occasions, such as the lunar New Year; in places our route lay under awnings made of the inside of oyster-shells that reduced still further the filtered sunshine of Canton streets, many here and there divided by wooden barriers with shoulder-broad gates as a protection against fires, or riots, or what not; finally a last bridge with an outlook suggestive of Venice, still more so at low tide to the olfactory nerves, and we broke out upon an untended open space across which was home.

In Canton where thieves are legion and beggars and food-hunting curs even more plenteous, yet where the heat is often intense, there are sliding doors of upright poles, so that while marauders cannot break in and steal, the family can sit inside in airy comfort, working, smoking, playing mah-jongg, quite indifferent to the comprehensive views of the sometimes picturesque domestic life within that is offered the passer-by. We lived in a proud residential section, too, or at least went through one on our way home, with such names as Many Impressions Great Street, in which still lived not a few rich people in the Cantonese sense of the word. Now and then we passed an open house-door with a coffin inside, right center, as it were, at one side of the room, the ancestral tablet straight back from the door, tables with food in front of it, people in white clothes bowing and scraping. Or it might be a bigger house dimly lighted with candles, priests in their two-color robes of office, like an Episcopal surplice, not too recently laundered, standing in formation, chanting, to the accompaniment of instrumental music. White and blue cloths would be draped over the street outside, the door flanked by immense paper lanterns, lighted by night. Sometimes these things remained the full hundred days of acute mourning, sometimes they were put up for a week or two and then taken down, to appear again toward the end of the hundred days, for most such things were rented for funerals, as similar ones, including most of the wedding presents, are for marriages.

We were struck by the number of funerals during our short winter in Canton. Smallpox was not rare; even some of our foreign community died of it; or perhaps many hurried up funerals that had been put off, in order to have them over with the sinister Year of the Pig and start anew with the luck-bringing Year of the Rat and a new cycle of Cathay. The whole families dressed in white, the women even with white in their hair, but sometimes only a small boy was left to do the real worshiping of the departed and the ancestors in general, for mere women cannot appease the spirits of the dead, much as they are expected to honor and feed them. Along the wide *ma-lu* of the once walled city a Chinese funeral with all its barbaric noises and colors looked out of place, but out here in the narrow, Confucian streets of our quarter it seemed in keeping. The one was as natural as a peasant burning joss and bowing down to the floor in a temple; the other was as incongruous as the man I once saw in foreign dress and of evident Western training kowtowing in his back yard before an up-to-date photograph of his father and offering the hungry spirit of the deceased old gentleman a bowl of American apples. The ancient and the modern constantly rub elbows in Canton, as when coolies carrying a red bridal chair and its many appurtenances wear above their brilliant red jackets and ragged, once-blue trousers tropical helmets of khaki with bright red bands.

***

One night on our way home from a Chinese feast in a famous restaurant of our section we passed a long array of things to be burned at midnight at the grave of a rich man just passed away, and among them was an automobile, of frame and paper like the rest, of no familiar make, but in the darkness so lifelike that had our gathering not been so missionary in atmosphere some one of us might easily have stepped into it with the Canton variation of "Home, James." A chauffeur and a high-class servant sat with respectful stiffness in the front seat, and in the back was a lovely lady in the richest garb, with a gay umbrella and glistening jewels; for according to the Chinese a man needs a woman quite as much as servants and food and transport in the after-world. All these, too, would be burned, victims to a cruel old Chinese custom – tremble not, for they were only of paper. The most Cantonese touch was a paper Italian flag flying from the front of the paper automobile. The friendly fellow who showed us all about the streetful of false things he had been set to guard could not explain nationality; to him the human race consisted of Chinese and outside barbarians; but he seemed to think that a foreign flag would be useful in the next world as in this, against property-confiscating generals and *Tuchuns*, and no doubt the Italian banner had appealed to his taste or to the available material.[52]

The months we spent in Canton seemed to be the wedding time of year, for we were constantly hearing the fire-crackers of jollification and finding mat-covered structures over the streets on our way home, such a *peng*, rented also, signifying that the house within had added a new bride to its ancient family line, and sometimes remaining a week or so more while musical celebrations day after day went on within.[53] But of course, there are more weddings in China than in our Western lands. In the first place everyone gets married, most of them early and many of the men often, and no one trusts his future to a colorless justice of the peace or city-hall clerk;

---

52 *Tuchun* = warlord. The foreign troops stationed on Shameen referred to them as "doojoons".

53 *Peng* = woven bamboo mats.

besides, guessy statisticians have been telling us for several generations that there are four hundred million people in the Celestial Empire.[54]

We lived not far from Laichee-wan, a park named for the chief fruit of the Cantonese region.[55] As a park it was much run down, but there you could see solemn old men, all the way from small merchants to the banker, come with their birds in cages from which they removed the cloth covers and, hanging them from a limb, let the captives sing for an hour or two while they themselves meditated and perhaps smoked. The Chinese do not keep dogs, in our Western sense of that verb, but they are inordinately fond of feathered pets. Now and again one met a rich man's aviary, half a dozen – in one case I met ten – servants in a row each carrying one of those

---

54 It is interesting that Franck is somewhat dismissive of the infamous "400 million" population figure in the mid-1920s. In his 2011 book *A Passion for Facts: Social Surveys and the Construction of the Chinese Nation State, 1900-1949* (University of California Press), the academic Tong Lam quotes the American diplomat John Watson Foster using the 400 million number in 1903. The Chinese too, both late Qing and Republicans, adopted the 400 million estimate which was being regularly used up until 1949. Tong Lam calls the 400 million estimate an "enumerative imaginery".

55 Laichee-wan is now the Lizhiwan Scenic Area, located in the old town of Xiguan. Laichee being more commonly lychee *(Litchi chinensis)*.

very high cages made in Canton to give birds as much flying-room as possible; but no man, however rich and important, scorned to bring birdy out for an airing himself if he had the time. There are Chinese who keep thrushes in cages and say it is a fine bird, not if it sings, but if it fights well. Most of our Canton neighbors, however, had more aesthetic tastes.

On the subject of keeping birds in cages, the rich comprador of the most important British bank in China had one of his homes within shouting-distance of our third-story windows, an immense establishment all but surrounded by canals as by a moat, and in contrast to the Italian-Chinese architecture of the rest of the estate he had erected overhanging a canal a house for his favorite wife, a "frame" house such as one sees nowhere in China, not merely all of wood but with clapboards and shingles, wooden "stoop" and blinds, altogether the most incongruous thing in Canton, an "American-style" house according to the husband, whose early-day travels in the United States had evidently been confined to rural parts.[56] The man himself lived in Hong Kong now, like so many of the rich men of Canton under Sun Yat-sen, for fear of

56 By "Italian-Chinese" style of architecture Franck is referring to those Western-style properties in Xiguan that fall into the new Baroque, neoclassical, tropical veranda, and pseudo-Gothic styles.

kidnapping and kindred troubles, doubled later when he was charged with a conspiracy to drive out the terror of the Manchus. But the favorite wife would not, I believe, have been molested in her clapboard love-nest if she had chosen to give her master a furlough and return to it; that seems to be one of the few ways in which the Chinese do not often try to injure the enemies.

***

Now that the walls were down we could walk directly from our suburb into the long, narrow, shaded shopping streets of all Canton, and see a thousand forms of handicraft and medieval merchandising. There are long streets of embroidery-shops, where men and boys and a few women sit before brilliant cloths stretched in horizontal frames and decorate not only garments but those pictures in embroidery so prized as gifts among the Chinese. "Artists" sit before crude easels in the doors of other shops, daubing leisurely but ceaselessly, apparently oblivious to the ever-changing crowd that is forever looking on. "Blackwood-furniture Street" offers everything in that line known to China, from mahogany to more polished pine knots, from those carved partitions used in the best houses to baby-carriages delivered at your door for the equivalent of an American half-dollar. In another street a vista of straw sandals stretches to infinity; in that, the "oyster-shell" windows and roof-extensions that help Canton to escape the sun are made of what are really huge clam-shells sawed as thin as isinglass and translucent, if not transparent; beyond, knife-handles, spoons, and a host of trinkets are fashioned from mother-of-pearl; horns of cattle or the water-buffalo are turned into lanterns; glass bangles and bracelets of imitation jade, wigs, mustaches, beads *(sic)*, no doubt for actors, switches made by the same men are laid out in heterogenous displays; for a hundred yards heaps of brass filings and a tendency for the teeth to stand on edge mark the making of the brass padlocks of China, in which the key is pushed rather than turned; silks, curios, mere junk – there is no end to the displays that crowd close on either side. Nothing is wasted; old electric-light bulbs are made into little goldfish bowls; rags are pasted in layers to take the place of leather; perhaps the two outstanding features of the crafts of China are their home-work, handwork in public and the immense amount of labor that is wasted on materials that cannot last long enough to be worth it.

One street in our suburb was given over entirely to silk-shops, a dozen polished men sitting ready to serve you; in China such places have several times more clerks than customers. Here are shops selling sandalwood, bits in the rough which people take home to burn to the household gods, some made into carved boxes, some into the frames of peacock-feather fans; farther on are fans of rooster-feathers, of mere paper, elaborately decorated or merely scrawled with a few Chinese characters, fans of everything from which a fan could possibly be made, whole streets in which you can pick up every manner of junk, new or second-hand, all those innumerable useless trinkets of which the Chinese are so fond. A dismal little alley facing the compound wall of the French Cathedral is almost the ivory center of China.[57] Here six, ten, sometimes a full dozen ivory spheres are intricately carved one inside the other, the outer one no larger than a billiard-ball, often, to the never-ending surprise of the foreigner, by mere boys who nonchalantly whittle away as if they were merely playing. One sees a few real elephant tusks, too few it seems, until one realizes that a single tusk may yield more than two hundred pounds of ivory. Even these dirty little dens open onto the street, and youths chisel away on the precious material right beside shops where the shin-bones of cattle furnish the "ivory". But one soon learns to recognize the peculiar grain of the real thing, and a few places in Ivory Street have a trustworthy reputation.

Nor will at least the feminine stroller overlook the pins, brooches, and other forms of personal adornment made of kingfisher feathers, once used as a sign of royalty under

---

57 The all-granite Gothic-style Sacred Heart Cathedral (1863) on the north bank of the Pearl River.

the Mongols and forbidden to the ordinary people. The dainty feathers of those vivid little streaks of blue that one so often sees flit across a rice-field are laid out and treated with some preparation that gives them the appearance of being enameled, while the bird itself no doubt is eaten. The more materially minded will note rough burlap bags of cattle-bones and masses of hogs' bristles just as they come from the butcher-shop in the doorways of other establishments given over to the making of toothbrushes. Old women wash the bristles, weigh, and tie them together in little bundles, clipping the ends off evenly. Men and boys saw up the bones, and when these have been polished and perforated with rows of little holes, women and girls take bunches of the bristles in their teeth to compact them, and sew them in.

Here too, and in adjoining narrower streets are the makers of mah-jongg sets – in northern mandarin "ma-chow" or "ma-chang," according to the French of Indo-China "matchang," in Canton "ma-cheuk"; suit yourself; by whatever name you call them the two characters stand for a kind of hemp and a species of sparrow that feeds upon it. Shanghai and other cities are more given to this trade than Canton, but even here it flourishes, for whatever their status now in fad-pursuing Western lands one still hears the bird-decorated dominoes clicking all night in houses and hotels everywhere in China that the game is not forbidden, as they did decades ago and no doubt will in decades to come. The "ivory" is prepared by sawing up the bones of cattle that have come to a violent if natural end. There is a greater market for bones in China than in the chicken-raisingest county in America, and one of the many ways your Chinese servant augments a meagre income is by selling these, along with tin cans, bottles, and other by-products of the kitchen scornfully discarded by the Western housewife.

The mah-jongg maker works entirely free-hand, like so many of his fellow craftsmen, sawing the bones, as well as the bamboo from farther south, on crude wooden frames with miniature buck-saws, tiny streams of water falling upon the growing fissures. Then mere boys, more often than men, standing or sitting facing the swarming street, stamp the figures, four Chinese points of the compass, and all the rest, and cut them out deftly with triangular-pointed chisels on bamboo handles, boring depressions in them with the simple bit, manipulated with a cross-piece and a spinning string, that is used for all such purposes in China.

Here are hundreds of ordinary-looking fellows, wearing only a pair of blue cotton trousers most of the year, producing marvelous bits of wood-carving with only rough patterns, or none at all, seeming to be left mainly to their own ingenuity, yet producing things as intricate as the world has to offer. The minute subdivision of the Canton trades is suggested by the fact that among the city's seventy-two ancient *hongs* or guilds one is of dealers in articles made of pear-tree wood.

***

Strikes were the order of the day. The recent victory of the seamen's union over the Government of Hong Kong had greatly emboldened the unions of Canton.[58] Just then it was the unloaders of rice-boats that were striking. Formerly every boat-load had given one sack of rice as a kind of squeeze to be divided between the rice-dealer and the unloading coolies. Now the unloaders demanded it all; also there was a question of the sweepings!

It was our luck to have left Canton before the "Shameen strike," but no harm is done by getting ahead of my story. The French governor of Indo-China and a large suite went to Japan ostensibly to pin on some ribbons and be pinned in turn. On the way home they went up to Canton and a big dinner was given them at the only hotel Shameen boasts. In the midst of it someone threw a bomb, not in the form of after-dinner pyrotechnics but of the literal, material kind, through a convenient window into the assembly. The governor-general was of course untouched; so were all his suite. But several members of the permanent

58   See footnote 5.

French colony, unimportant persons on the edge of the festivities, were killed or injured. Nor was it surprising that an Annamese whose body was found floating in the river a few days later should have been found guilty of the crime, just as the perpetrators of outrage against Japanese officials anywhere are always *ipso facto* Koreans.

The governor did not make a hundred-per-cent impression among at least the Anglo-Saxons by hurrying away next morning without waiting to see how the score of injured French residents came out or to attend the funeral of the three men and two women killed. Urgent affairs of state called him back to Hanoi forthwith.[59] The British consul ran true to form in harshly interpreting his bounden duty; the authorities of Shameen, startled into a realization of the long-evident fact that the rule about Chinese not being permitted on the island except for proper reasons was being loosely enforced, ordered that henceforth no "outside resident" was to be admitted after 9:30 at night without a pass from the foreign functionaries. There was also, I believe, some requirement of the photograph of the pass-holder, which would of course have been necessary to enforce the order.

---

59   For more on the June 1924 bomb incident on Shamian Island see Paul French, 'Blast from the Past', *South China Morning Post Weekend Magazine*, November 20, 2022.

Chinese had long been accustomed to use the Shameen Bund as a place to sit and chatter in the evening, rather than make a clean, untroubled gathering place of their own. Led by the comprador of the Canton branch of a large American firm, all Chinese engaged on the island struck. Not a bank bookkeeper, clerk, policeman, coolies, cook, "boy", ama *(sic)*, or any other variety of Chinese, postal employees excepted, would set foot upon the island.[60] British and American business men, never before seen at anything harder than holding down a desk-chair and perhaps elevating a cocktail-glass or a tennis racket, had to put on khaki trousers and unload with their own fair hands the food supplies that came up from Hong Kong. They city merchants would not sell to Shameen residents; or if they did, there was no one to carry the stuff to the island. Sun Yat-sen was accused of stirring up the people against the foreigners, to whom he had not been showing full brotherly love.

The strikers said that they had nothing against foreigners elsewhere in Canton; the difficulty was to prove oneself no Shameener. If kind-hearted people out at Tung Shan or across the river at Paak Hok Tung or down at the "C.C.C." tried to help by inviting the island aristocrats

---

60   More commonly "amah". An amah or ayah is a girl or woman employed by a family to clean, look after children, and perform other domestic tasks.

to meals, their servants threatened to strike also.[61] The fact that they were acting less from choice than from compulsion did not help matters. Rickshaw-men began to refuse to pull foreigners, whatever their residence. The American consulate had to get its meals from gunboats in the harbor. Foreign gunboats had to be used to carry men on important missions. The strike extended to all British business men; the foreign steamers from Hong Kong had to stop running because no Chinese would unload them at Canton and no Chinese would travel on them, and the few foreign passengers did not pay for the fuel the engines consumed. The Chinese boats would not take foreign passengers; the railway to Kowloon had been broken for years.[62] The strike lasted for seven weeks, and a thorough Chinese strike is no laughing matter. When at last it was settled, the authorities of Shameen knew how it feels to climb down off a high horse.

***

Kidnapping being a favorite Chinese sport, it was surprising to find no apparent tendency to steal the children of foreigners, surely a rich possibility. Some of the crimes might have been imported from our own cities, as when two men posing as electric-light inspectors

---

61   The CCC being the Canton Coolie Corps.
62   The Kowloon-Canton Railway (KCR).

were let into the home of well-to-do people near us and proceeded to rob them. The little boy of the family came home just then, sized up the situation with Chinese quickness, and got the police. The sequel had nothing in common with New York; no bail, no lawyers, no expert alienists, no months of delay, no acquittal or insufficient evidence or reversal of the decision by a high court because a "t" thereof had not been crossed. The men were paraded through the streets for a few hours as soon as an announcement of their crime could be hastily written and appended to them, and then were shot out in the open space in front of our gate, left there the rest of the day with the same rude placard still beside them, and toward dusk were carried away in slap-dash coffins. Let a man so much as steal a gold bangle from a sing-song girl and he was shot before the sun set, or rose, as the case might be – unless he happened to have special influence with the military. The mayor of Canton, who was none other than Sun Fo, only son of Sun Yat-sen, petitioned the "Generalissimo," to wit, his famous father, through official channels and the public prints, not to let the soldiers shoot men in the public streets; but as we shall see in due season the poor old gentleman did not have much authority in his declining days over the hordes he had brought in to bolster up his precarious cause.[63] But

---

63   For Sun Fo see footnote 48.

even though there were unpleasant sights and sounds, the foreigner really had less reason to worry about his wife and children anywhere in the streets of Canton than in any one of the first hundred American cities.

***

Perhaps it was because we still had Peking and Nanking in mind that we found Canton by no means so large a city, in extent at least, as we had expected.[64] We could walk in an hour from the further edge of the western suburb to the ancient Five-Story Pagoda on the northernmost corner of what was for centuries the city wall.[65] We used to like to wander there, not only because it was the only remnant of the old barrier that was still shrinking and yielding its ancient materials to new use, but because of the view it gave of all the city and much beyond. Tumbled masses of what had once been great concrete forts over which Sun Yat-sen and one of his former pals had fought desperately two or three years before were excellent examples of the effect of shell-fire, though they had been chiefly overthrown by hand and dynamite in the interests

64   Nanking = Nanjing.
65   The Ming-dynasty Zhenhai Tower (1380) was the northernmost watchtower of the old city wall. It is now within Yuexiu Park in central Guangzhou and houses the Guangzhou Museum.

of more civic improvements. A big Western-style park had already been completed at the foot of the hill, and the plan was to include this within it.[66] The most famous old landmark of Canton, much more truly of five stories than a pagoda, was only a wreck of its former self, ready to fall at a heavy shake, and rumors were persistent that it was to be razed also, like so many of the ancient monuments of Canton. Dr. Sun has assured us in person that it would be preserved, repaired, and made a part of the new park system; but unless the work goes on apace, which is not likely with political conditions what they have been of late years, the thing will soon fall or blow over of its own decrepitude.[67]

Looking out across compact Canton from Five-Story Pagoda Hill and the last remnant of the city wall the eye caught first the Flowery Pagoda in the back foreground, with the "British yamen" a big blotch of green close beside it, on the sky-line the twin spires of the French cathedral and, farther to the right, past the wireless towers recently erected on the Bund of the "southern capital," the great department-store down on the busiest part of the river-

66 Yuexiu Park, also known as Yut Sau Shan, Yut Sau Hill or Mount Yuexiu, once formed the northern end of the former walled city.

67 The pagoda was eventually rebuilt in 1928. Sun Yat-sen did not live to see the restoration.

front, with here and there a pawnbroker's tower, perhaps as far away as Honam.[68]

For several years just before our Civil War, Canton was held by a British and French garrison, as a result of the second "opium war," and during that time the two nations saw no harm in solidifying their positions there.[69] The French confiscated a group of official buildings from which the occupants had fled and erected the cathedral that, until the recent flurry in department-stores, towered above all else in the city, which was not only bad joss, according to the geomancers, but a typically Gallic bit of arrogance. The British naturally could not do without their share, so they occupied another big cluster of official buildings just across the narrow street from the Flowery Pagoda, which to this day is known as the "British yamen."[70] Standing in the heart of land-hungry Canton, a great green splotch of huge old trees hiding a few half-ruins, yet which no Chinese can enter, it seems at the least out of date. Nor do the British make any great use of it. Belonging to the foreign office in England but rented to the Hong Kong Government as a lodging for

---

68   The Five-Storey Pagoda is located in Yuexiu Park.

69   American Civil War 1861-1865; Second Opium War 1856-1860.

70   A "yamen" usually meaning a headquarters or residence of a Chinese government official or department.

its student interpreters, it is no one's business to keep the place up; and though it is half the size of Shameen, there are only a few habitable rooms, and Hong Kong has to rent other lodgings for some of its young hopefuls, that they may learn the language they so promptly forget after they return to the little colony as "civil servants."[71] For there it is naturally impossible for them to associate with the "natives" even in order to keep up what they have so laboriously and expensively acquired, and the case is not unusual of young Englishmen who have spent two years studying the dialect of Canton and Hong Kong using an interpreter in all their official dealings with the race under them. In fact the then minister of education of Hong Kong, who had learned Cantonese as a student interpreter twenty-five years before, now spoke only pidgin English to his "boy."

Not far from the one called flowery is what is popularly known as the "smooth pagoda."[72] Like a big factory chimney tapering toward the top, it is really the minaret

---

71   Student interpreters were entry-level positions in the British diplomatic and consular service, principally in China, but also in Japan and the Kingdom of Siam (Thailand). Student interpreters normally remained such for a number of years within established embassies and consulates. Many later rose to senior diplomatic positions.

72   A common name for the Huaisheng Mosque, on Guangta Road, built in 850 and reconstructed in 1468. As it is not

of the little mosque in which some of the Mussulmans of Canton still meet on Friday afternoons. Arab traders seem to have found their way to this great port long before the days of Marco Polo, long indeed before it was really a Chinese city. Outside what used to be the North Gate of Canton, in a cemetery of Chinese Mohammedans, there still stood when we were there – one must be cautious in speaking of anything destructible that is within the power of the southern generals – the large-domed tomb, like those of Damascus, of what is reputed to be a maternal uncle of Mohammed himself, who, Hwei-hwei legend has it, migrated to China soon after the Hegira. [73]

The once famous City of the Dead beyond consists now mainly of coffin-boards built into huts and used as ditch-bridges. The Canton of Sun Yat-sen has little sympathy for the old superstitions. Yet all about the city, among the rice-lands, the orange-, laichee-, and mulberry-groves in which a toiling multitude works from dawn to dark, are scattered burial-places for the dead.[74] Particularly Paak Wan Shan, the big heap of hills east of the city that do

---

adorned by any decoration it acquired the nickname of the "Smooth Pagoda".

73   Mussulmans/Mohammedans: Muslims. In AD 622, the prophet Muhammad completed his Hegira, or "flight," from Mecca to Medina to escape persecution.

74   Laichee: lychee.

not always belie their name as the abiding place of white clouds, is covered high and low, far and wide – hills to blue distance and the surrounding ridges as far as the eye can see – with myriads of the horseshoe-shaped concrete graves of southern China, of all sizes and ranging from gleaming white to weather-blackened, according to the occupant's wealth and date of burial. It is a popular day's excursion, safe enough ordinarily even for foreign ladies, and coming back one is almost sure to meet a big funeral wailing its winding way through the garden-fields, and certainly a lone pair of gaunt coolies carrying to the lower foothills the remains of a child or of a mere soldier in the thinnest of pine coffins.

A unique feature of the Canton landscape and district round about is the pawnbrokers' tower-warehouses that bulk everywhere high above the surrounding buildings. Huge, solid, square blocks of masonry, most of them age-blackened, with tiny windows and even those subdivided by bars, though it is like dissecting a flea, they are a constant reminder of the dangers to property in this region. In times of peril – that is, most of the time nowadays – the wealthy pawn their valuables, less for need of ready cash than for safe-keeping. These places are particularly numerous on the Honam side of the river – which reminds me that Canton may seem smaller than one expected partly because the eye takes in little more than the solid waterfront of that great compact section of it half-way across the Chu-kiang.[75]

HONAM

Honam ("south of the river") is a large island in the Pearl River, its upper nose an important part of the city of Canton, its lower end at Whampoa an hour by steamer below. Constant strings of sampans ferry the population back and forth, and the steamers from Hong Kong and elsewhere come and go on the farther side of the island when the tide is low enough to show the two reefs marked with red lighthouses just off Dutch Folly.[76] It is a wonderful river, by the way, not yet fished out for all the crowded population that has fed upon it for so many centuries, so that men fish with nets right off the swarming Bund, like the Frenchmen on the Seine quays of Paris, with the difference that the Cantonese seem now and then to be rewarded for their trouble.

When those five *ma-lu* with which the municipality threatens to cut up our suburb of Saikwan are finished there are to be others in Honam, but meanwhile it is as

75 The Zhujiang, or more commonly in English, the Canton or Pearl River.

76 See footnote 31.

puzzling a labyrinth of emaciated lanes as you will find in China. Honam makes much matting, or rather, it stencils in fancy colors on matting sent in from the country districts where a simple frame and some bobbins thrown incessantly back and forth across it turns reeds into these Chinese substitutes for mattresses and rugs. Most of the famous "Canton china" comes from Honam also, and that, too, is not really made there but in Kingtehchen, home of Chinese porcelain.[77] It comes to Canton in big baskets "from Kiangsi," as the local workers put it, the province being as far as their geographical knowledge carries. How disturbed the country has been of late is shown by the fact that this unfinished china, which for centuries came overland by river-boats and coolie carriers along an old imperial trail, now goes all the way round through Shanghai and Hong Kong by sea, at of course several times greater cost. Men trot through the streets of Honam, not with "biscuit," but with baskets of once-baked china covered with a white glaze, and there it is painted in the gaudy styles that represent Canton's ideas of decoration. There is grinding of colors here, too, but the blind are not employed at it; probably there is hardly work for all those with full faculties. The kilns in which the colors are baked on are small, and the sweat-shop

---

77   The famous "dragon kilns" of Jingdezhen in northeastern Kiangsi (Jiangxi) province.

conditions under which some women and many rather elderly men paint and live in dark and dismal holes would probably disgust even Kingtehchen.

There is an important highway, as southern China understands the word, along Honam Island from its crowded Canton suburb to the Canton Christian College, an establishment, like several other of our mission institutions in China, better off in buildings, equipment, and no doubt personnel than many an American college at home.[78] It is a winding flagstone trail, hardly four feet wide, and in places raised well above the fields, for which the nose is often duly grateful. The fertility of the small but endless gardens of Honam is largely due to hundreds of jarfuls of that which so frequently brings distress to the nostrils in rural China, but here, especially in the morning, even on New Year's day, there was a strong counter-scent of green onions in the air, as great bundles of these, of garlic, of those long-stemmed cabbages widely cultivated by the Chinese came trotting into town on coolie shoulders. The "road" passes close behind the well-guarded cement factory in which the "Generalissimo"

---

78   Founded by American Presbyterian missionaries in 1888 and later to become part of Lingnan University in 1916. It relocated to Macao for a period due to its suppression by the Qing authorities but returned to Canton in 1904. Franck is referring to the building by its old name in the 1920s.

had his headquarters and refuge, and under the edge of a small real-estate-boom town of returned Chinese from America, with some imposing looking houses of American pattern, cement sidewalks, but grass roads between them, and a name suggestive of Bible-reading, Cherith.

The Chinese are tireless in watering their fields, or in doing anything else that will make their crops a little better, and those about Canton are constantly being sprinkled by coolies and peasants who carry all day long from the nearest water-hole two big wooden buckets with long spouts. But it is really night-soil, even the night-water, on which they chiefly depend.[79] For in China nothing is lost. To fatten the impoverished soil they conserve carefully every fertilizing particle, so that the earth itself, like the thick air of the narrow city streets, is saturated with the refuse of humanity.

***

Not far behind the Canton Christian College is an old temple among trees on a hill, where a former bartender in America lives as a priest. A man of seventy-five now, he went to California at twenty, worked as a house-boy in San Francisco, tended bar in Phoenix, Arizona, and brought back as his chief memory of the United States an insatiable taste for chocolate cake. He keeps Chinese

---

79   Faeces and urine.

wine, which he offers, in cups that do not speak well of his dish-washing abroad, to all foreigners who drift up to his retreat, meanwhile chattering fluently in terrible English; and his definition of a gentleman is one who takes "only two or three fingers." Upon his return to his native land he gave all his money to the monastery he now inhabits, on condition of being well taken care of until death, properly buried, and joss generously burned to his spirit – but just then the call of "Dinner! Come and get it," sounded in its Cantonese equivalent, and he bade us a hasty au revoir.

The story of Honam would be incomplete without mention of its biggest man, Lei Fuk-lum. Some miles still further out beyond the college by another flagstone trail he has built himself a feudal castle, with moat, drawbridge, loopholes for the rifles of its many defenders and all the rest. In his early days Lei Fuk-lum was a bandit who held up many gambling-games and other places of sudden revenue, especially illegal ones, with no other weapon than a small blackened lamp-chimney, wherefore he is known as "Lamp-chimney Lei" – Canton's mispronunciation of the good old Chinese family name Li.[80] Legend has him

---

80   General Lei Fuk Lam (aka, and now more commonly, Li Fulin – 1872/1874-1952) was born in Panyu County (now Zhuhai) to a peasant family. After a military career he became governor of Honam (Honan) Island, and later took charge of

a kind of Robin Hood, robbing the rich, the gambling halls, and the like partly to give to the poor. Gradually he came to be the real boss of all Honam Island, with its seventy-two villages and perhaps 300,000 people, was officially made so under the Manchus, and has held it to this day, with the title of general – perhaps marshal by now – under every rival holder of Canton since the revolution.

He wears an eye-filling uniform, keeps a crowd of armed ragamuffins close about his person, has a sizable army of his own, and at his yamen, a former temple in the most crowded part of the Honam suburb of Canton, dispenses justice and its antithesis like an old ward-heeler of Tammany in its halcyon days.

From the turreted top of Lei's castle his guards can look far away across the flat country, though with hills in both directions, Whampoa and the two pagodas, some of the

---

the city government as mayor, and was military governor of Kwangtung Province, which transferred to Honan when the Yunnanese took control of the city proper. This period lasted until late 1927. Additionally he was a patron of the Canton Christian College. Shortly after Franck was resident in Canton, in December 1923, Lei was elected by Cantonese troops in the pro-Sun Yat-sen army as their representative. As such he went to Hong Kong in an attempt to enter into peace negotiations with the Kwangtung Army. In 1949 Lei left Canton for Hong Kong where he lived until he died.

river itself, in plain sight. The place is surrounded by a great orange-orchard in which ripe fruit hung heavy on that New Year's day, and the master's orders seem to be to give to any respectable-looking visitors, foreigners included, all the sweet oranges they can eat and carry away. The moat was almost a lake, the great concrete house sitting in the middle of it impregnable to anything but heavy artillery. Flowers bloomed wherever there was space for them; a guest-room well separated from the rest of the house proved that the general took no foolish chances. But the men on guard, with alert eyes and ears rather than with guns, made no protest when we strolled about the very restricted grounds, and even a few of his wives came down to peer at us through the slight shrubbery. Lei follows the convenient plan of keeping a wife or two wherever he may need one, rather than toting them about with him. So absolutely did he command the island that even the "C.C.C." depends upon him for order and keeps in his good graces.

There is another pleasant walk from the college across the island, though with such wandering among grave-lands and through several villages that the most astute evil spirit could never hope to follow. An occasional childish cry of *"Fang gwai-lo!"* – Cantonese for *yang gwei-tze*, or foreign devil – greets the stroller, with hints that the scamps are being egged on by whispering adults. One comes out on the further branch of the river, opposite Paak Hok Tung – White Crane Grotto, though I have never seen any of the three there – with other big mission schools and a foreign residence suburb which considers itself the safest of all from stray bullets during the constant civil wars.[81] A small boat largely taken up by the family altar will set one across, unless the wind is too high; and if the legs are still willing not to fall back upon the launch to Shameen, one can wander on along more winding stone roads through green and scented vegetable-gardens and several villages to Fati, with other foreign residences.[82] In fact, if all the foreign communities scattered about Canton, the original home of foreign trade and Protestant missions in China, were gathered together in one town, Shameen, the hub of them all, would indeed be a little island by comparison.

Fati has many flower-gardens, with trees and shrubs bound into those dwarfed and crippled forms into which the Chinese, though less so perhaps than the Japanese, are given to training decorative plants that to the Westerner

---

81   Also known as Paak Hok Tong. The local mission schools included the Women's School (also known as the True Light Seminary) and the Bible Women's School, both funded by the American Presbyterian Church.

82   Fati, aka Fa Ti, Fe Tee and now more commonly Fangcun District, to the southwest of the city centre, was an area noted for its market gardens, plant nurseries and ornamental tree vendors.

would be more beautiful in their natural shapes and forms, something akin perhaps to binding the feet. Some of these flowering shrubs are fitted up with painted heads and hands of baked mud to suggest Buddhas or ancient worthies.

Here too, one sees many of those glazed earthenware seats, in rich blue and the like, which the wealthy scatter about their gardens. A little farther on is the station of the shortest of Canton's three railway lines, to Samshui, thirty miles away on the West River, with stations almost every mile, but only two cities, notably Fatshan, the Newark of South China, second in population only to Canton itself, though little known abroad.[83] From the station one of a hundred contending boats, almost certainly manned by women and children, will carry one back across the river above the island that divides it into less dangerous width on those many days when the winds sweep up through the "Macao passage" to the nests of "flower boats" at the entrance to our creek, with the third railway station nearby. That is the line northward that hopes some day to join Hankow-Peking at the Yang Tze, and perhaps even have a connecting loop with that from Kowloon, so that our grandchildren may be able to board a train across the harbour from Hong Kong and get out of it at Peking. But

---

83 Samshui now being Sanshui District, a part of Fatshan, Foshan City.

much water will probably flow under the old humped stone bridges of China before that day comes – and it will take away some of the charm of China as a half-impassable country.

APPENDIX

Roving Through Southern China: The Photographs

The photographs accompanying this text were all taken by Harry A Franck himself. As well as a prolific writer and diarist, Franck was a copious photographer. His archive at his alma mater, the University of Michigan, runs fully to 9,056 black-and-white images and an additional 1,001 colour photographs. Many of the colour images are hand-tinted lantern slides on glass that Franck prepared himself to illustrate his lectures. They largely retain his own hand-written image descriptions.

Some nitrate film stock has disintegrated over the years and been lost, but the vast majority of his lifelong output of photographs and lantern slides remain to be viewed at the Special Collections Research Center, University of Michigan Library, at Ann Arbor, along with ancillary materials including correspondence, manuscripts, drafts, lectures, journals and scrapbooks.

The publishers were often impressed by Franck's photography and included more than the average number of photographs in most of his books – adding the marketing note that the books included 'unusual photographs by the author'. *Roving Through Southern China* contains fully 171 photographs by Franck, a largely unprecedented number of images to be included in a book in the mid-1920s.

However, examining some photographs, it is clear that Franck provided only brief descriptions while it appears that he could not read Chinese. For instance, one photograph in his collection included in *Roving Through Southern China* is simply titled as "a yamen" (being the administrative office or residence of a local bureaucrat or mandarin in imperial China) though it clearly displays a sign in Chinese for a "lycee" or school. Indeed, it is the well-known Guangdong Province First Middle School (now the Guangdong Guangya High School). Though it may well have been originally constructed as a yamen, it was a school at the time Franck photographed it. A minor quibble, but relevant to the historians examining his archive perhaps.

Also available in the *China Revisited* series:

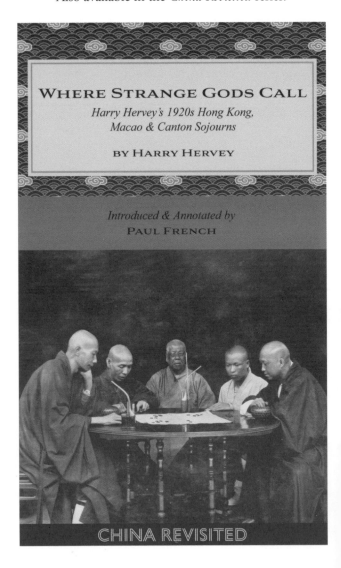

WHERE STRANGE GODS CALL

*Harry Hervey's 1920s Hong Kong,
Macao & Canton Sojourns*

BY HARRY HERVEY

Introduced & Annotated by
PAUL FRENCH

CHINA REVISITED

WANDERINGS IN CHINA

Hong Kong & Canton
Christmas & New Year 1878/1879

BY CONSTANCE GORDON-CUMMING

Introduced & Annotated by
PAUL FRENCH

CHINA REVISITED

LING-NAM

Hong Kong, Canton &
Hainan Island in the 1880s

BY BENJAMIN COUCH "BC" HENRY

Introduced & Annotated by
PAUL FRENCH

CHINA REVISITED